PHUKET

PHUKET

William Warren

Photography by
Luca Invernizzi Tettoni
and Alberto Cassio

ASIA BOOKS

One of the many isolated islands that dot the seas surrounding Phuket

© 1992, 1991, 1989, 1987 Pacific Rim Press (HK) Ltd
Published and distributed by Asia Books Co.,
5 Sukhumvit Road Soi 61,
Bangkok 10110, Thailand,
P.O. Box 40
Tel. 391-2680, 392-0910, 392-8049
Fax. (662) 381-1621, 391-2277

All rights reserved. No part of this book may be produced, stored in a retrieval system, or transmitted in any form, or by any means, electronic, mechanical, photocopying or otherwise, without the prior permission from the Publisher.

Whilst every care is taken in compiling the text, neither the Publisher nor the Author or their respective agents shall be responsible for any loss or damage occasioned by any error or misleading information contained therein or therefrom.

Special thanks to the Tourism Authority of Thailand (TAT), especially Khun Mana Chobthum and Khun Jitkasem Boonthong of the Phuket TAT office for their invaluable assistance.

Photographs by Luca Invernizzi Tettoni 5, 17, 18, 19, 20, 22, 25, 27, 28, 46, 56-7, 59, 60-1, 62, 63, 67, 69, 72, 76, 78-9, 81, 82, 83, 84, 86, 92, 93, 94-5, 97, 98, 101, 103, 108, 110-111, 123, 125, 129, 138; Alberto Cassio 7, 33, 38-9, 40, 47, 52, 54, 58, 66, 74, 87, 96, 100, 105, 120, 142; Helka Ahokas 6, 43, 48, 68, 70 (bottom), 80, 82, 90, 91, 106, 116-117, 127, 132, 136-7; Michael Freeman 70 (top); Ashley J Boyd 89

Editor: Richard Lair
Project Editor: Christopher C Burt
Photo Editor: Caroline Robertson
Design: Unity Design Studio
Cover concept: Raquel Jaramillo and Aubrey Tse
Maps: Winnie Sung

Production House: Twin Age Limited, Hong Kong
Printed in Hong Kong by Sing Cheong Printing Co., Ltd.

Koh Phi Phi Ley

Contents

Introduction	**8**
Getting there	8
Climate	8
Swimming hazards	8
Transportation on the island	14
Etiquette	14
Hospitals	15
Shopping	15
Outside communications	15
History	**18**
Phuket Today	**24**
Beaches	**29**
Mai Khao and Nai Yang Beach	30
Nai Thon Beach	30
Bang Tao Beach	30
Pansea Beach	32
Surin Beach	32
Kamala Beach	32
Patong Beach	34
Karon Beach	40
Kata Beach	43
Nai Han Beach	44
Rawai Beach	44
Away from the Beach	**47**
Phuket Town	47
Port of Phuket	49
Khao Phra Thaeo National Park	49
Aquarium	53
Laem Phrom Thep	53
Phuket Museum	53
Wat Chalong	53
Wat Phra Thong	53
Lak Muang	53
Chinese Temples	55
Sea Gypsy Village	55

The art of displaying food

Thai Boxing	55
Phuket Golf and Country Club	55
Yupadeewan Nursery	55
Muslim Villages	55

From Phuket by Land 63

From Phuket by Boat 64
Phi Phi Islands	64
Phang Nga	75
Koh Pannyi	80
Other islands near Phuket	82

More distant excursions 88
Similan Islands	88
Krabi	88
Tarutao National Park	92

Cultivated Plants of Phuket 93

Festivals and Holidays 107
National Holidays	107
Vegetarian Festival	112

Useful Information and Addresses	118
Other Publications	134
Vocabulary	138
Index	143

Special Topics
Bird's Nest Soup	69
Pearl Farming	85
Eating Thai (with a southern accent)	102
Sea Gypsies	104
A Poet on Phuket	115

Maps
Phuket Island	10
Thailand	12
Northern Beaches	31
Patong Beach	35
Karon and Kata Beaches	42
Nai Han and Rawai Beaches	45
Phuket Town	50
Koh Phi Phi Island	65

Introduction

Getting There

The Thai Airways International Company has several flights a day between Bangkok and Phuket, the number depending on the season (extra flights are often added for holidays); the trip takes just over an hour. In addition, Thai also has direct flights to Chiang Mai thrice weekly. Tradewinds, a new airline owned by Singapore Airlines, has daily direct flights to/from Singapore and Dragon Air operates daily to/from Hong Kong. Kuala Lumpur and Penang are serviced by Thai as well. During peak months—November through February—planes are usually full, so be sure to reconfirm your return flight; Thai Airways has a special window at the Phuket airport for reconfirmations.

There is no railway to Phuket, though it is possible to take the train to Surat Thani and then take a five-hour taxi ride. Air-conditioned tour buses offer over-night service from Phuket to Bangkok, taking about 14 hours with meals served en route. Cheaper, non-air-conditioned buses make the same trip daily. (For travel information details, see pages 130–132.)

Climate

Phuket lies near the equator, and temperature ranges are slight throughout the year; the average minimum is around 25 degrees, while the maximum is 31 degrees. There is a perceptible rise in March and April, the hottest months, and a drop in December, though it never gets really cool.

Rainfall is irregular and unevenly distributed, totalling about 2,200 mm. (90 in.) a year, but generally the wettest period is between late May and late October, when the western coast receives the full force of the monsoon, and the driest is from November until mid-March. From March through May rainfall tends to be localized and usually falls in the late afternoon, thus never seriously threatening a holiday by the sea; even as late as August it is possible to spend a week on the island without encountering too many rainy days. The island lies outside the path of typhoons and other major tropical storms.

Swimming Hazards

While Phuket's beaches are generally safe, one should be aware of the dangers of undertow, especially during the monsoon season. Undertow is most hazardous at high tides during the period of the new and full moons. Since conditions vary from place to place and season to season, visitors should ask and heed the advice of responsible local people.

(Life-saving hint: if you should find yourself pulled offshore, don't panic and try to 'fight' your way back in; let the current pull you up or down the beach and sooner or later a counter-current will help push you back in.) Sharks are quite rare and do not pose a risk. Schools of small, stinging jellyfish sometimes appear after strong winds from the sea, but these rarely stay more than a day or so.

Phuket at a Glance

Size:
550 sq. km (212 sq. miles) plus another 49 sq. km (19 sq. miles) including surrounding islands. Highest point 532 m. (1,622 ft.).

Location:
Off the west coast of the Kra Isthmus of Thailand lying between 7° 30′ and 8° 10′ latitude north and 98° 15′ and 98° 30′ longitude east.

Population:
Approximately 180,000 (1989 estimate) of which about 50,000 live in Phuket town.
—60% Thai, Thai-Chinese Buddhists
—35% Thai Muslims
—5% Moken (Sea Gypsies)

Per capita income:
Approximately US$3,000 per annum (Second highest in Thailand). National average approximately US$800 per annum.

Land use:

Rubber	15,000 ha	27.0% of area
Coconut	5,000 ha	9.0% of area
Forest	4,400 ha	7.2% of area
Orchard	3,000 ha	5.0% of area
Rice paddy	2,200 ha	3.7% of area
Pineapple	800 ha	
Durian	500 ha	
Cacao	90 ha	
Palm oil	70 ha	

Tin mining operations occupy much of the remaining surface area.

Phuket harbors approximately 350 industrially-equipped fishing boats which employ around 10,000 people full time, either processing or fishing.

Tourism:
Over 800,000 foreign tourists visited Phuket in 1989, up from 42,000 only seven years previous in 1982, West Germans led the total, followed by British, Hong Kong residents, Australians and French.

Phuket Island

Map of Thailand

Phuket's Size in Relation to Other Islands of the World

Manhattan (U.S.A)	52 sq. kl.	(22 sq. miles)
Hong Kong Island	94 sq. kl.	(36 sq. miles)
Elba	224 sq. kl.	(86 sq. miles)
Malta	247 sq. kl.	(95 sq. miles)
Koh Samui (Thailand)	250 sq. kl.	(96 sq. miles)
Penang (Malaysia)	266 sq. kl.	(110 sq. miles)
Isle of Wight (U.K.)	382 sq. kl.	(147 sq. miles)
Barbados (W. Indies)	432 sq. kl.	(166 sq. miles)
Phuket	**550 sq. kl.**	**(212 sq. miles)**
Corfu (Mediterranean)	595 sq. kl.	(229 sq. miles)
Singapore	621 sq. kl.	(239 sq. miles)
Tahiti	1,045 sq. kl.	(402 sq. miles)
Oahu (Hawaii)	1,542 sq. kl.	(593 sq. miles)
Bali (Indonesia)	5,582 sq. kl.	(2,147 sq. miles)

Climate Table

		J	F	M	A	M	J	J	A	S	O	N	D	Ann.
Phuket Town	Avg. Temp. F.	79	80	82	83	82	82	81	81	80	80	80	79	81
	Avg. Temp. C.	26	27	28	28	28	28	28	27	27	27	27	26	27
	Avg. Precip In.	1.4	1.1	2.6	5.9	11.0	11.8	11.1	10.9	12.9	14.3	8.1	2.7	93.8
	Avg. Precip mm.	35	28	66	150	279	299	282	277	329	364	206	69	2384
Phang Nga	Avg. Temp. F.	73	78	83	86	85	83	81	81	81	80	77	73	80
	Avg. Temp. C.	23	25	28	30	30	28	27	27	27	27	25	23	27
	Avg. Precip In.	1.4	3.0	5.1	9.8	12.7	18.5	15.5	16.9	17.5	13.6	7.5	3.4	124.9
	Avg. Precip mm.	35	76	130	249	323	470	394	429	445	355	190	86	3182

Transportation on the Island

Phuket has no regular public transportation system with scheduled routes and times, and while there are taxis in town and at some of the larger resort hotels they still tend to be rare. The most common method of getting around is by mini-bus (called *song taew*), which serve most of the beaches, normally using the terminus near the public market in town. (What this means, in practice, is that to get from Kata Yai to Nai Harn, only two beaches apart along the rugged coastline, one may have to go all the way into town on one song taew and then take another to the final destination. This annoyance will probably change as the new ring road nears completion.)

Each mini-bus holds five or six people on a first-come, first-serve basis, and fares range from around 15 to 40 Baht depending on the distance. It is wise to ascertain the fare before getting on. Service stops around 6 in the afternoon, when the last ones leave for the market, so any visitor planning an evening away from the beach where he or she is staying should arrange for alternative transport. (See pages 122–126 for detailed travel information.)

Jeeps and motorbikes are available for rent at most of the popular beaches. When hiring vehicles, remember that Thais drive on the left side of the road and that negotiating the steep, twisting roads requires skill and reliable brakes.

Etiquette

Thais are extraordinarily tolerant when it comes to putting up with alien behavior, but for good relations it would be wise to observe local customs and try to conform with them. In daily life, the Thai ideal is a 'cool heart' (*chai yen*) which means avoidance of extremes such as overt displays of emotion. The fact that even Thais do not always achieve it does not lessen its importance; thus anger, however justified by Western standards, rarely produces the desired result. Excessive shows of affection are also considered improper. Proper decorum is particularly important in places of worship, whether Buddhist, Chinese or Muslim, not only in behavior but also in dress; a good general rule to follow is to observe the local people and follow their examples. Shorts and 'tank tops' are not suitable for visiting temples.

Nude bathing is officially frowned upon and should be avoided, at least on those beaches used by Thai tourists, which means most of the larger ones on Phuket.

Hospitals

Phuket has good hospitals if medical attention is required. The Mission Hospital, on Thepkasatri Road in town (telephone: 211173) has an English-speaking staff; others are Phuket Ruamphaet Hospital on Phuket Road (telephone: 216179), and Siriroj Hospital on Krabi Road (telephone: 215666).

Shopping

Such is the efficiency of commerce in present-day Thailand that umbrellas and wood-carvings from the far north are commonplace in the shops of Phuket. The best buys, however, are batiks from neighboring Malaysia and locally-made goods, particularly those utilizing sea-shells and bamboo. Sea-shells have been turned into just about every conceivable kind of decorative item, from picture frames to lamps; rare shells are also available for the serious collector. The greatest concentration of shops selling such goods is in town, but Phuket Sea Shell, just opposite the entrance to the Phuket Island Resort, is worth a special visit because of its exceptionally large range of products.

There are two or three antique shops downtown. The prices tend to be higher than those in Bangkok or Chiang Mai and a sizeable proportion of the 'antiques' are of recent origin, but occasionally it is possible to find good specimens of old water jars with Chinese designs on them.

Cashew nuts are also a good Phuket bargain, being considerably cheaper here than in Bangkok. Buy them in town, if possible, rather than at airport shops where prices are inflated. At most shops, bargaining is not only permissible but expected. (For list of shops, see page 133-134)

Outside Communications

Several of the larger beach hotels offer telex and long-distance telephone services. Otherwise, there is a central telephone exchange in town near the post office. Radio telephones are still the only form of outside communications from Karon and Kata beaches as well as Phi Phi Island. (See page 126)

The sun sets slowly over a beach in Phuket

TOURIST ARRIVALS — 1989

Nationality	Total	Jan.	Feb.	Mar.	Apr.	May	Jun.	Jul.	Aug.	Sep.	Oct.	Nov.	Dec.
Thai	216851	18333	17934	20248	22282	21329	14665	16221	15978	15161	21101	16635	16964
U.S.A.	32281	3049	2847	3449	2806	2411	1616	2254	2097	1962	2690	3661	3439
Canada	13928	1669	1599	1730	1352	539	538	716	704	685	1201	1610	1585
Austria	10997	1788	1527	1373	710	398	379	363	296	372	702	1452	1637
Belgium	4515	673	548	325	360	193	129	466	297	186	221	529	588
Denmark	4332	414	406	404	317	120	209	616	210	275	377	327	657
France	39719	6451	5280	4640	2848	1540	1030	1653	3476	926	2024	4594	5257
W. Germany	74748	10263	9516	8450	5679	3087	2084	3166	2894	2367	6045	10132	11065
Italy	32411	6446	5373	2613	1973	1026	1003	965	4147	1142	1813	2389	3521
Netherlands	4126	503	330	409	245	153	183	246	417	270	283	415	672
Sweden	8377	1137	960	644	812	376	444	338	388	518	628	1164	968
Switzerland	24565	4115	2826	2268	1815	916	724	1054	888	788	2192	3160	3819
U.K.	55284	5044	5341	5116	5009	2917	2753	4021	4204	3331	4406	7168	5972
Middle East	2410	317	247	213	160	155	88	268	180	148	252	198	184
Australia	42194	4320	2942	3655	4057	3305	2816	3864	2962	3278	4231	3354	3410
Hong Kong	46484	2897	5425	4158	3726	2645	3623	4374	5330	3561	3662	3120	3963
Japan	22863	1667	1554	1810	1283	1448	1154	2480	3854	2015	1654	1608	2336
New Zealand	4216	487	301	404	414	274	132	318	441	308	298	341	498
Taiwan	26515	1870	2150	2007	1807	1022	1238	2838	3364	2327	2635	2300	2957
Malaysia	12380	756	1159	1136	1132	1316	950	884	818	758	651	1142	1678
Singapore	26296	1583	1996	1986	1668	2055	3482	1840	1420	1432	2088	2426	4322
Others	20681	1821	1342	1241	1551	1118	1125	1648	2919	1096	2102	2389	2329
Total	726173	75603	71603	68281	62006	48341	40365	50603	57284	42896	61256	70114	77821

History

"Between Mergee and Jonkcelaon there are several good harbours for shipping, but the sea coast is very thin of inhabitants, because there are great numbers of Freebooters, called Saleiters, who inhabit islands along the sea coast and they both rob and take people for slaves and transport them for Atchen and there make sale of them and jonkcelaon often feels the weight of their depredations."

Thus wrote one Captain Hamilton, an English adventurer familiar with the Bay of Bengal in the latter part of the 17th century. Translated into modern geographical terms, "Mergee" was Mergui, now on the southern coast of Burma but then belonging to the Thai Kingdom of Ayutthaya; "Jonkcelaon", which also appears in early writings as "Janselone" and "Junkceylon" was the island now known as Phuket, at that time a tributary of Ayutthaya but semi-independent due to its distance from the capital. (The name Phuket, sometimes spelled Bhuket, is derived from the Malay word *bukit*, meaning "hill" or "elevation", a reference to its mountainous terrain.)

Little is known about the earliest days of Phuket's history, though there is evidence of neolithic habitation north of the island at Takua Pa, as well as in the bays of Phang Nga and Krabi. Under various names Phuket was known to ancient voyagers from India, China, Arabia, and eventually Europe, but for a long time there were no

An early European trader's map designating Phuket as Junk Seilon

permanent trading posts. Among the first settlers were the semi-nomadic sailors known by present-day Thais as Chao Nam, or 'water people', also sometimes called sea gypsies. These people of uncertain racial origin probably were the Saleiters of Captain Hamilton's description, whose piratical lifestyle terrorized sailors along the coast until they were finally suppressed by the English in the 19th century; their descendents can still be seen around Phuket today, bold-eyed people known for their willingness to take on risky jobs like deep-sea diving and climbing to the heights of vast limestone caves.

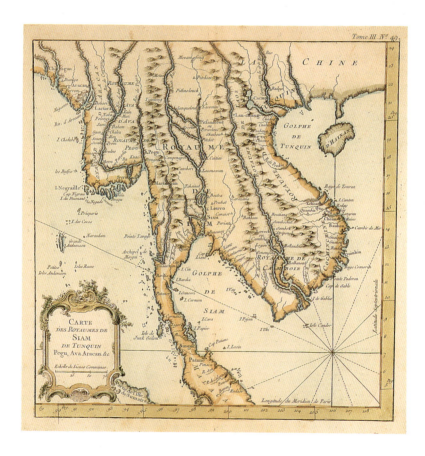

Very early in its history, the source of Phuket's eventual prosperity was discovered. This was tin, which was so plentiful that it could be easily extracted from veins near the surface in seemingly endless quantities, and which was as valuable in the ancient worlds as it continues to be in modern times. Other rare commodities were available on the island or the nearby mainland: ambergris, rhinoceros horn, ivory, and rare forms of coral. An exotic item was edible birds' nests; deposited by tiny swifts in lofty caves, these nests were much esteemed by the Chinese for their supposed medicinal and aphrodisiac qualities. On the walls of one of the largest birds' nest caves, on the nearby island of Koh Phi Phi, there are paintings of Chinese junks which took part in the trade as long ago as the Sung Dynasty.

The Thais reached the far south during the reign of King Ramkhamhaeng of Sukhothai, in the late 13th century, but for a long time their power remained tenuous, partly because of the distance involved and partly, no doubt, because of the fierce Chao Nam. Gradually, though, the northerners organized the region, and in the Ayutthaya period, which started in 1350, Phuket with its wealth of natural resources was assigned to the same *monthon*, or administrative area, as Nakorn Sri Thammarat, which had a long cultural history as a center of the great Srivijaya Kingdom.

Soon after Vasco da Gama discovered the sea route to India in the early 16th century, Europeans arrived to exploit the riches of the region previously controlled mainly by Arab traders. Siam was in a

unique position to profit from these newcomers since at that time it was the only country in the East in possession of tin mines, the richest of which were on Phuket. Export of the metal became a royal monopoly, and the island itself was placed under the immediate control of the central government.

Simon de la Loubere, who headed a French Embassy to Ayutthaya in 1687, mentioned Phuket in a book he later published about his experiences; he noted that the islanders were granted the privilege of working their own mines, paying a royalty to the king in the form of a share of their produce. La Loubere also records that a French medical missionary named Brother Rene Charbonneau served as Governor of the island from around 1681 to 1685, an appointment that may have been devised by the Thais as a means of thwarting the designs of other European countries.

In 1689, following a revolution in Ayutthaya that resulted in the expulsion or imprisonment of most Europeans, French forces from Pondicherry threatened to retaliate by occupying Phuket. General Desfarges, who had formerly commanded French troops in Ayutthaya and also at a small but strategic trading post on the Chao Phya River called Bangkok, arrived at the island with 332 men, hoping to frighten the Thais into allowing his fellow Frenchmen to extract enough tin from the mines to compensate for losses suffered in the anti-foreign uprising.

When the Thais refused to cooperate, Desfarges decided to retreat for fear that continued hostilities would mean death for some 70 Europeans still held captive in the capital; he later perished in a storm just off the Breton coast on his homeward voyage.

Phuket next entered the pages of history in the early years of the Bangkok period. Having destroyed Ayutthaya in 1767, Burma was once more threatening the kingdom and enjoying a series of victories in the south in 1785. An army proceeded to lay siege to Thalang, then Phuket's principal town, and for a time the situation seemed desperate, especially when the Governor suddenly died. Fortunately, the Governor's wife, Chan and her equally redoubtable sister, Mook, took charge of the defences. According to Sir Arthur Payne, an English historian, "They assembled men and built two large stockades wherewith to protect the town. The dowager governess and her maiden sister displayed great bravery, and fearlessly faced the enemy. They urged the officials and people, both males and females, to fire the ordnance and muskets, and led them day after day in sorties out of the stockades to fight the Burmese. So the latter were unable to reduce the town and after a month's vain attempts, provisions failing them, they had to withdraw."

In reward for their service, King Rama I of Bangkok conferred a title of nobility on Chan, who became the Lady Tepsatri, while Mook became Tao Srisuntorn. Statues honoring these two heroines now stand in a prominent position on the road leading into modern Phuket from the airport, near the site of their brave stand.

Near the statues can be found the Lak Muang, an ancient pillar of phallic aspect which marked the center of the island and served as its spiritual guardian; many Phuket residents still come to make offerings and to pray for favors ranging from success in love to a winning ticket in the national lottery. Thalang, however, ceased to be the island's main settlement, which shifted south to the Kathu Basin at a port (formerly known as Thung Ka) on Chalong Bay.

Shortly before these stirring events, Phuket narrowly escaped becoming a British possession. Captain Francis Light, a British trader of considerable influence, spent several years on the island and, in 1772, married one of its inhabitants. Aware of the strategic advantages of Phuket and Penang, further down the coast, he recommended acquisition of both islands; the British government, however,

eventually opted for Penang only, and Phuket remained Thai.

In the 19th century, as the threat of foreign invasion subsided and the rapacious pirates were brought under control, Phuket's economy flourished. Tin was still the main source of prosperity, and the labour force swelled with the arrival of thousands of Chinese miners, some from nearby Malaysia and some all the way from China itself. During the reign of King Rama V, in the second half of the century, an estimated 30,000 Chinese were employed by mines scattered over the island. Diligent and hard-working, some became wealthy mine-owners themselves and built splendid mansions that still grace the scenery.

Malays also came and established a strong Muslim presence on the island, occasionally coming into conflict with the increasingly powerful Chinese. After one serious uprising, arbitrators came from China to settle the dispute and restore peace.

Toward the end of the 19th century, King Rama V himself visited Phuket, thus dramatizing the island's importance to the central government of Siam. Phuket, as well as Phang Nga and Krabi on the mainland, were entrusted to a notable Governor named Theapibal Rasada, who held office from 1890 to 1909 and who is credited with many innovative developments. In 1903 the first rubber trees were planted, beginning a major new industry that would transform Phuket's agriculture and add greatly to its prosperity. The town of Phuket grew rapidly, its streets lined with handsome buildings in a Sino-Portuguese style inspired by those of Malacca, and ships from all over the world called at its bustling port. In 1933, the island officially became a separate province.

Despite all these developments, and despite the fact that until recently Phuket regularly contributed more than any other province to the national revenue, it remained for many years relatively isolated. Roads in southern Thailand were scarce and often impassable during the rainy season, and the island was accessible only by boat, primarily from Krabi. The trip was thus a long and arduous journey for residents of the capital, few of whom could claim to have visited Phuket as late as the 1960s. A major highway system, the opening of regular air service, and most of all, the Sarasin Bridge connecting the island with the mainland dramatically changed this state of affairs. In the mid-70s, *Newsweek* magazine, in a special feature, listed Phuket as a destination for travellers seeking something special and undiscovered; within a short time, more and more tourists had discovered its idyllic beaches and a significant new industry was born. A Bangkok travel agent was quoted in 1977 as saying, "The South is the coming place. A few years ago hardly anyone had ever heard of it. Now everyone wants to go there."

Phuket Today

Covering an area of some 550 square kilometers, Phuket measures 50 kilometers from north to south. Good roads lead to most of the island's beaches, and a ring road currently under construction will eventually cut travelling time between beaches by a considerable degree; at present though, the hub of communication is the provincial capital, and it takes longer than one might expect to cover a relatively short distance as the crow flies. The terrain is hilly, sometimes almost mountainous, especially in the south where granite cliffs as high as 160 meters thrust dramatically into the Andaman Sea to form bays, where the best beaches are located.

The dense jungle that once covered the major part of the island is now largely gone, except for one area near the old town of Thalang; this forest, which has been preserved as a national park is centered around a granite outcropping called Khao Phra Thaeo. Here towering trees still form a natural canopy over lush tropical foliage, picturesque waterfalls cascade down the rocky slopes, and gibbons and exotic birds can be glimpsed in the higher branches. Elsewhere, sadly, the valleys and flat areas have been cleared for mining or agriculture.

Phuket's population is estimated at around 180,000 though this is growing rapidly due to an influx of newcomers, some from as far away as distant Chiang Mai, who come to participate in the tourist industry. The greatest concentration, about 50,000, is in the provincial capital Phuket Town, a thriving center where new buildings seem to be going up everywhere to alter the leisurely charm of the not too distant past. Many of the elegant old Sino-Portuguese mansions and private homes remain, however, the houses often set in spacious gardens shaded by lofty mangosteen trees. Another survivor, the stately building that houses the District Office, evokes a nostalgic ambiance which earned it a role as the French Embassy in Phom Penh during the filming of *The Killing Fields* several years ago.

In terms of race and religion, Phuket's people are varied. Buddhists constitute the majority, probably about 60 percent; besides ethnic Thais this group includes numerous assimilated Chinese, who have traditionally dominated the island's economy. There are also Thai Muslims, estimated at around 35 percent, as well as a sprinkling of Malays, Indians, non-assimilated Chinese, Pakistanis, Europeans, and the Mokens, or so-called "sea gypsies". In 1980, the island had 28 Buddhist temples, 29 mosques, four Christian churches, one Sikh temple and a dozen or so Chinese temples.

Important as the tourist industry has become, it is by no means the sole, or even the primary, source of the island's current prosperity. Phuket's per capita income exceeds that of any other Thai province; it

rose from 17,357 Baht in 1976 to 39,376 Baht in 1980 and is almost double that today. Tin mining continues to be scarcer, although as surface deposits are becoming exhausted, off-shore dredging is increasingly important. Rubber is the major cultivated crop, and much of the arable land is devoted to plantations that often climb up hillsides. The Thai government maintains a rubber research station on the island to develop higher-yielding trees and offers various incentives to growers to encourage them to gradually replace older plantings with new plants. During the seven years it takes for a growing tree to reach the stage when it can be tapped, the area is often intercropped with pineapple, in the production of which Thailand has become one of the world's leaders.

Coconut plantations are also common, and an estimated 30 million nuts a year are harvested, often with the aid of trained monkeys which scamper up the lofty trees and throw the ripe ones down. Phuket is also noted for its cashews; on the island these are not grown in large plantations, as they normally are on the mainland, but almost every compound contains a few trees. The cashew tree (botanically related to the mango) bear globular red fruit with a single nut hanging pendant-like from the bottom. Other local fruits include the celebrated durian, passionately praised by its admirers, as well as jackfruit, rambutan, mangosteen, mango, and a long somewhat bitter bean called sato, which is regarded as a delicacy in southern cuisine. There are commercial plantings of oil palms and, a more recent introduction, cacao.

Rice fields can still be seen in the flat lands but far less so than in the past since they are increasingly being turned into more profitable orchards or, near the sea, resort facilities; most of the rice consumed in Phuket today comes from neighboring provinces.

Additional wealth comes from the sea in the form of fish, crabs, lobsters, and rare shells; pearl farming, though still in its experimental stages, is also practised. Some of the off-shore islands, especially around Koh Phi Phi, contain huge limestone caves, the upper reaches of which are the favoured haunts of a tiny swift that constructs its nest on the cave walls. These nests are mostly composed of a saliva-like secretion that hardens on exposure to the air; they constitute the main ingredient of the famous bird's nest soup, treasured for centuries by Chinese gourmets for reputed aphrodisiac and medicinal qualities. The government strictly controls nest collection, awarding contracts only to firms who return part of their profits for conservation and agree to harvest selectively so as to protect the bird.

Prosperous as it is, Phuket nevertheless faces a number of challenges, with old ways of life rapidly changing and the future not

altogether clear. Tourism has brought new sources of income, but it has also brought the dangers of uncontrolled development and a despoiled environment. Anyone who knew the island even a few years ago is surprised, not always pleasantly, by the rapid 'progress' on once pristine bays. Aware of the problems, the government has launched a number of ambitious programs, among them dams and reservoirs to increase water supply, new roads to facilitate communication, replanting of areas deforested by mining, and a master plan for developing tourist facilities.

Thanks to its long-established traditions and economic infrastructure, Phuket appears to stand a better chance than many other resort areas of winning the battle and of retaining its fabled charm and natural beauty.

Beaches

All of Phuket's best beaches lie on the western side of the island facing the Andaman Sea. Extending from Mai Khao near the airport to Rawai at the southern tip, there are a total of some 13 western beaches, not counting small coves inaccessible except by trails. A decade or so ago, the southern beaches were practically cut off by the high, rocky ridges that rise along the coast and jut out into the sea to form isolated bays, each with its own unique ambiance. Today roads lead to the larger beaches though it is still necessary to make long inland detours to reach some of them. A coastal road presently under construction will eventually make it possible to travel from beach to beach without going inland and also gain some spectacular seascapes.

Looking at a map, one might deduce an equal profusion of beautiful beaches on the east coast. Most of these, however, are fringed by impenetrable mangrove swamps, and other have been defaced by off-shore dredging for tin, making them unsuitable for recreation.

The first beach to be 'discovered' by international travellers was Patong, about 20 years ago, and its stretch of white sand was soon overlooked by a string of simple thatched-roof bungalows. The real boom in resort facilities began less than 10 years ago, and now there are hotels and/or bungalow complexes on every beach of any size, rising with such speed that any list would be incomplete by the time it was published. Yet despite this proliferation, each cove manages to retain its distinctive character and it is still possible for a visitor to select the one that meets his or her own particular escapist needs.

The following is a survey of the main beaches and their accommodations, starting with the northernmost. (Please note that accommodation prices are invariably negotiable or subject to 'low season' discounts as well as tax and service surcharges. Below is an explanation of our hotel cost rating system. Prices are for a standard double room:

****	2,500 Baht up (very expensive)
***	1,500–2,499 Baht (expensive)
**	500–1,499 Baht (moderate)
*	under 500 Baht (inexpensive)

25 Baht = US$1

Mai Khao and Nai Yang Beaches

Most planes fly over Mai Khao Beach when landing at Phuket's airport. Mai Khao together with Nai Yang Beach forms a 10 mile stretch of sand. At low tide the sea can be muddy compared with the translucent water further south and partly for this reason it is less popular with tourists. Another reason is that the shore drops steeply into deeper levels, creating unpredictable and hazardous water currents during the monsoon season. Nai Yang is noted for its impressive casuarina trees and is a popular picnic spot with Thais, part of it having been designated as a national park; a few bungalows are available, as well as facilities for bathing after a swim. Both beaches are notable for being favored destinations of the giant sea turtles which come ashore to lay their eggs in the sand between October and the end of January.

There are no accommodations on Mai Khao beach, making it a pleasant day trip destination for those seeking a truly pristine beach setting.

Nai Yang beach accommodations consist of tents and simple government-run bungalows which can be rented for 60 Baht (tent for two persons) to 500 Baht (bungalow for 12 persons) from the Royal Forest Department office; enquire at the Tourist Authority of Thailand (T.A.T) office in town for details. There is also the plush **Pearl Village Beach Hotel** at the southern end of Nai Yang Beach. The 163 rooms are set in 20 acres of landscaped gardens. Room rates range from 1,500 Baht (single) and 1,700 Baht (twin) to 9,000 Baht for the 'Pearl Suite.' (Plus 21% tax and service surcharge.) Tel. 311338-9.

Nai Thon Beach

This is a quiet beach with a fishing village and few tourist accommodations. Exposed to the full force of the monsoon, it is not too popular with swimmers, though it has a bucolic charm and will probably attract further development in the future.

Bang Tao Beach

This long sweeping beach is still largely undeveloped for tourism with the exception of the 240 room **Dusit Laguna Hotel**, a fine property which shares the beach with a small fishing village. The Dusit Laguna costs 1,815 Baht for singles up to 8,470 Baht for its suites. Tel. (076) 311320-9.

However, a 250 room Sheraton Hotel is currently under construction as well as the Pacific Islands Club, which will feature on 18-hole golf course. Both are scheduled to open in 1992.

Northern Beaches

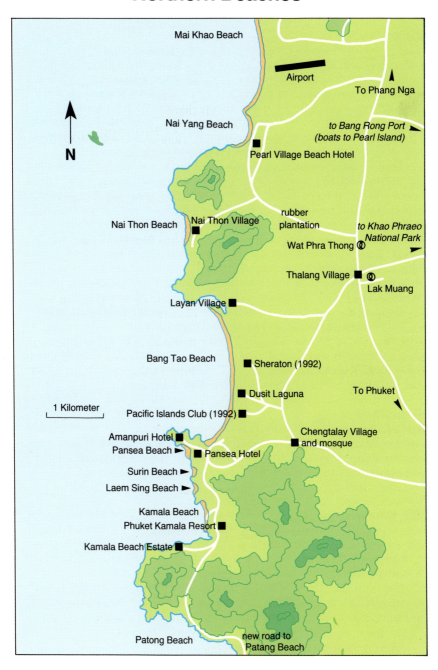

Pansea Beach
This is one of Phuket's loveliest beaches in terms of scenery, with good snorkeling and swimming during the dry season. It can be rough in the rainy months, however, with a strong undertow, and caution is advised for visitors at that time as is true for all of Phuket's western beaches. Dominating Pansea Beach is the Pansea Hotel. With its bucolic atmosphere and recently renovated 'nipa-style' huts, the Pansea is Phuket's most romantic beach accommodation. You can actually fall asleep to the sound of waves breaking on the beach, something the airconditioned-cement-block hotels elsewhere can't offer. There are 110 cottages spread over its 10 acre property as well as a library, games room and video room (sorry, no TVs in the rooms). A Chinese junk makes day and sunset cruises for 500–1,000 Baht per person including cocktails and snacks. Prices range from 4,000 Baht for a cottage including breakfast, 6,000 Baht for a three bed family cottage and 11,000 Baht for a suite cottage complex which sleeps up to ten people. This resort is highly recommended; most visitors return for more. Reservations should be made well in advance, tel. 311249 or fax (076) 311252.
   Right next door to the Pansea is the spectacular **Amanpuri Resort** — Asia's most exclusive and expensive resort hotel. The Amanpuri encompasses 40 private Thai-style pavilions nestled in a coconut plantation on its own beach. The design and fixtures are without equal on Phuket. Room rates start at 6,000 Baht up to 15,800 Baht per night. Tel. (076) 311394 or in Bangkok 250-0746.

Surin Beach
This is a popular beach with Thai day-trippers, especially on weekends and holidays. Steep hills rise sharply behind the sand and there is an equally sharp drop into deeper water, which makes swimming somewhat hazardous in the rainy season.

Kamala Beach
The natural beauty of this curving stretch of white sand has been marred by off-shore tin dredging, but the scenery is still impressive. It will almost certainly see future development.
   Currently there exists one accommodation, the Phuket Kamala Resort on the southern end of the beach. Their brochure notes, "Joyful both the skin dive and scuba, all comfort is waiting for you". Room rates range from Baht 900 during the low season (April–Sept) to Baht 1,800 in the high season.

Patong Beach

Some four kilometers long, Patong remains the most developed of all Phuket's beaches, almost solidly lined with hotels, bungalow complexes and a concentration of restaurants, shops, and night-spots appealing to all tastes. Not for those in search of tranquility, but definitely suitable for anyone wanting a lively holiday. Thus far the beach has remained remarkably clean, and the turquoise sea is a playground for all kinds of sports, among them wind-surfing and water scooters. The following is an almost comprehensive listing of Patong beach accommodations:

Ban Kosol Bungalow
Radootit Road
tel. 321195-6

**

62 rooms and bungalows. Although a bit far from the beach, this is a pleasant new addition to Patong Hotels.

Capricorn Bungalow
Radootit Road
tel. 321390

*

22 rooms. Nice accommodation under English management.

Club Andaman
Beach Road
tel. 321102
Bangkok tel. 2701627

**

128 rooms. Swimming pool, bar, restaurant and conference rooms.

Coconut Villa
Meridien Road
tel. 321161, 321160

*

39 rooms. Restaurant, short walk to the beach.

Coral Beach Hotel
South end of Patong Beach
tel. 321106-12

***

200 rooms. Has a lovely setting and layout. Not right on the beach, but within walking distance.

Diamond Cliff Resort
North end of Beach Road
tel. 321501-6

****

Opened 1988 and a bit overpriced considering its bad beach location.

Holiday Inn
Beach Road
tel. 321020

***

280 rooms. The usual fine quality of this international chain is well represented here.

Patong Beach

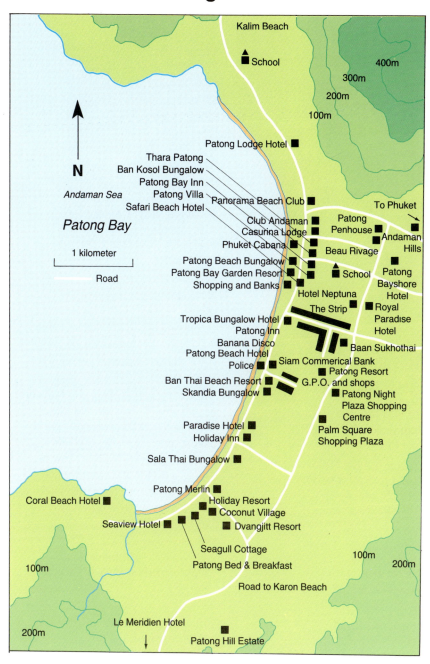

Holiday Resort
Meridien Road
tel. 321119

Panorama Beach Club
Road to Kalim Beach
tel. 321451

Paradise Bungalow
Beach Road
tel. 321172

Patong Bay Garden Resort (Also known as Patong Bay Hotel)
Beach Road
tel. 321297-8

Patong Bay Inn
Beach Road
tel. 321092-3

Patong Bayshore Hotel
On the Beach Road
tel. 321011-5

Patong Beach Hotel
Beach Road
tel. 321301-6
Bangkok tel. 2330420

Patong Lodge Hotel
Road to Kalim beach
tel. 321286-7

Patong Merlin Hotel
Beach Road
tel. 321070-4
Bangkok tel. 2532641-2

Patong Resort
Raj-Uthit Road
tel. 321333-5

**
105 rooms. Air-conditioned and fan. Auto rentals available.

**
43 fan and air-conditioned rooms. Shady setting near the beach at the Phuket Road junction.

*
20 fan and air-conditioned rooms.

**
46 rooms. Right on the beach with swimming pool and beachside restaurant. Nice family style resort.

*
36 rooms with air-conditioning or fan.

**
56 rooms. In Patong about as far from the bayshore as you can get.

**
122 rooms and bungalows. Patong Beach's first hotel and still one of the nicest, set in a coconut grove. Tennis court and discotheque.

***
46 rooms with air-conditioning, refrigerator, etc. Nicely isolated on the very northern end of Patong Beach.

***
297 rooms. Swimming pool. Pleasant restaurant with ocean view.

**
210 rooms. Set back off the 'strip', opened in 1987.

Patong Villa
Beach Road
tel. 321132-3

**
24 rooms with restaurant.

Phuket Cabana
Beach Road
tel. 321138-40
Bangkok tel. 2782239

***
75 rooms. On the beach with swimming pool.

Safari Beach Hotel
Beach Road
tel. 321230-1

**
40 rooms. Fitness center, T.V. in rooms. Next to the 'strip'.

Seagull Cottage
Beach Road
tel. 321238-40

**
56 rooms. Quiet setting on southern end of the beach with good ocean view and beach access. Second floor rooms are superior to the first floor.

Seaview Hotel
Beach Road
tel. 321103

**
74 rooms. Restaurant and nice quiet location near the beach.

Skandia Bungalows
Beach Road
tel. 321320

**
20 bungalows in Thai style. Scandinavian restaurant. A good value for the cost.

Thara Patong
Beach Road
tel. 321135, 321520

**
118 rooms and bungalows. One of the most recent openings in Patong.

Tropica Bungalows Hotel
Beach Road
tel. 321204-6

**
36 rooms. Right on the 'strip' in the middle of the town.

A fisherman casts his net at Ao Kata beach (left); Fishing boats lying idly upon Ao Rawai beach (top right); Nai Harn beach (bottom right)

Karon Beach

Karon actually consists of two beaches; a perfect little cove known as Karon Noi (and also, by some, as Relax Bay) and the much larger Karon Yai. Karon Noi is occupied entirely by the Le Meridien Hotel, while its bigger neighbor on the other side of a promontory has a choice of hostelries. There is good snorkeling around the coral reef of the promontory, and despite the new developments, both beaches are comparatively quiet. It should be noted, however, that of all the beaches on Phuket it is Karon beach which is developing the most rapidly. Beachfront property that sold for only 40,000 Baht per *rai* (about US$3,000 an acre) seven years ago now sells for 10 millon Baht (about US$750,000 per acre) now. At least ten new hotels popped up along the seafront here during 1986 alone.

Kakata Inn '85'
Karon Beach (south end)
(Also known as Kata Inn or Kata Inn '85')
tel. 214824–7 (town office)

**
50 fan rooms and bungalows. Lovely location right on the beach, pleasant but not very good restaurant. Currently under renovation.

Kata Villa
Karon Beach (south end)
tel. 381602

*
22 fan rooms and bungalows.

Karon Villa/Karon Royal Wing
Karon Beach (north end)
tel. 381149–55

****
152 rooms. The first luxury hotel on Karon beach with swimming pool, jogging track and all other standard amenities. Karan Royal Wing added in 1990.

Le Meridien Hotel (also known as the 'Relax Bay Resort')
Karon Noi Beach
tel. 321480–5
Bangkok tel. 2548147–50

****
470 rooms. One of Phuket's newest and most deluxe resorts. On its own beach with two swimming pools. Squash, tennis and other sports facilities. Superb cuisine as well.

Marina Cottage
Karon Beach (south end)
tel. 381625, 381516

**
56 rooms. Situated on the rocky bluff overlooking south Karon Beach. Picturesque cocktail bar above the beach.

Phuket Arcadia Hotel
Karon Beach
tel. 214841-2
Bangkok tel. 2547901-2

****

255 rooms. The Arcadia is a huge new Karon property that now dominates the otherwise low-key Karon Beach horizon.

Phuket Golden Sand Inn
Karon Beach
tel. 381493-5

**

50 rooms. Another of the recently opened up-market resorts of Karon beach. Very reasonable room rates.

Phuket Ocean Resort
Karon Beach (north end)

*

16 fan rooms.

Thavorn Palm Beach Hotel
Karon Beach (middle section)
tel. 214835-8

****

Another of the rather large new resort hotels of Karon Beach. 210 rooms and suites. All rooms with TV and refrigerator.

Karon, Kata and Kata Noi Beaches

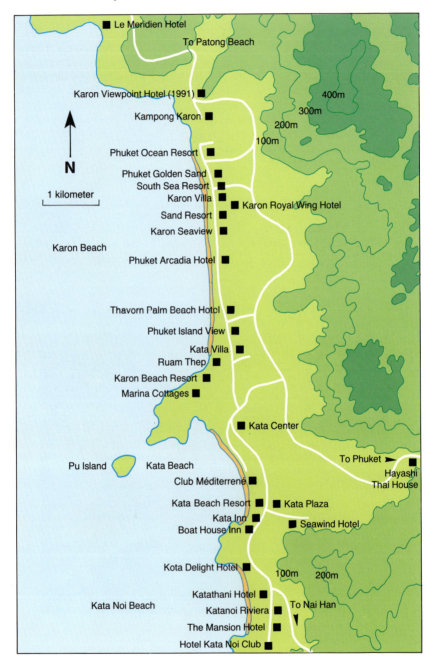

Kata Beach

Like Karon, Kata is separated by a prominence into Kata Yai ("Big Kata") and Kata Noi ("Little Kata"). The former is the site of the Club Mediterranee, which opened in 1986 and sprawls unobtrusively along most of the beach, although there are also a number of bungalow complexes as well as a more recent collection of bars and restaurants. The usually calm blue bay, graced by a romantic island, is popular with yachtsmen. Over the hill lies Kata Noi, site of the Kata Thani Hotel and bungalow complex, a small but exquisite beach with a dramatic backdrop of jungled hills.

The Boathouse Inn
Kata Beach
tel. 381557–60

**

36 rooms. Very pleasant are relatively in expensive. "A hotel for people who don't want to stay in hotels" as the owner says. Rates include meals.

Club Mediterranee
Kata Beach
tel. 381455–60
Bangkok tel. 2539780–4

***

300 rooms. Rates include all meals and facilities except drinks. Advance booking only.

Hyashi Thai House
Highest point along Karon-Phuket Road
tel. 381710–4
Bangkok tel. 2581928

***

50 rooms and bungalows. Built on a magnificent site of the top of the pass to Phuket Town. The best Japanese restaurant on Phuket is here.

Katathani Hotel
Kata Noi Beach
tel. 381417–25
Phang Nga Road

****
212 rooms. Best location on an exceptionally beautiful beach. Swimming pool, in-house video.

    Kata Noi beach has seen a proliferation of inexpensive bungalows developed over the past few years. These simple accommodations usually cost in the Baht 100–200 range.

Nai Han Beach
The road from Kata to Nai Han offers some of the most spectacular views in all of Phuket, climbing as it does over hills that reach 300 meters. Nai Han is the site of the deluxe Phuket Yacht Club, which rises up a hill at one end; otherwise this beach is relatively undeveloped. A number of hotels elsewhere on the island bring their guests here for a day of swimming and sun, and there are some excellent seafood restaurants along the shore. The sea shelf drops fairly abruptly, and swimmers should be careful during the monsoon season.

Phuket Yacht Club
Nai Han Beach
tel. 381156–63
Bangkok tel. 2514707, 2517059

****
108 rooms. One of Thailand's most sumptuous and expensive resorts. Beautiful layout and truly exceptional rooms and swimming pool. Worth a visit for a drink or just a look.

Rawai Beach
Though picturesque with its fringe of coconut palms and fishing boats, Rawai is a shallow, rather silty bay that makes it less popular with swimmers than those to the west. Nevertheless, it has a number of attractive bungalow complexes and transportation is available to nearby Nai Han for those who want more serious water sports. A community of sea gypsies lives at one end of Rawai.

Laem Ka Beach Inn
Laem Ka Beach
tel. 213799

*
Located about 1 km. east of Rawai Beach of Wiset Road.

Rawai Plaza and Bungalow
Rawai Beach
tel. 381346–7

**
50 fan and air conditioned bungalows. Located in a new shopping plaza.

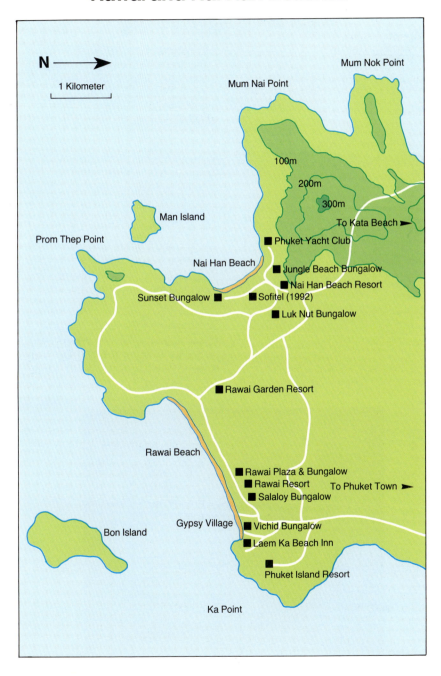

Phuket Island Resort
Laem Ka Beach
tel. 381010–7
Bangkok tel. 2525320–1

***
300 various types of rooms and bungalows. A bit far from the beach, 2–3 kilometers east of Rawai, Phuket's first luxury resort. Popular with tour groups and conventions.

Rawai Resort Hotel
Rawai Beach
tel. 212943

**
83 rooms. One of Phuket's first beach hotels. Shady, pleasant layout. Swimming pool.

Other accommodations near the Southern Beaches

Cape Panwa Sheraton
27 Moo 8 Sakidej Road
tel. 391123
Bangkok tel. 2363535

***
142 rooms. Lovely hotel by itself on a year-round safe beach off SE Phuket. Very good value for money. Coconut fringed beach.

Lone Island Resort
Lone Island (Accessible by boat from Chalong Bay)
tel. 381374, 381858

**
30 bungalows. Isolated on Lone Island, a place for those who want to get away from it all. Free boat transport. Must book in advance.

A view of Phuket Town from the Rang Hill Public Park

Away from the Beach

Sea and sand are the great lures for the average visitor to Phuket, but even the most dedicated sun-lover may occasionally want to escape the beach and explore the rest of the island. Here are a baker's dozen destinations for that morning or afternoon — or even that whole day — when sunburn or monsoon rain stirs a desire for alternative pleasures.

    Phuket Town Most roads, and all mini-bus transportation, lead sooner or later to the provincial capital, a bustling little city originally settled by Chinese from Malaysia about a century ago. Perhaps because of its origins, the atmosphere of the town is less Thai than Malay, with older buildings in the Sino-Portuguese style of Malacca and open storm drains along the arcaded streets. Today the drab and unimaginative *hong taew*, or 'row shop', predominates as it does in most Thai cities; but there are still grand old Chinese houses, often with elaborately carved doors and windows, to provide pleasant surprises during a stroll through the downtown area. The oldest public buildings are Government House, used as a locale in *The Killing Fields*, and across the road, the Provincial Court, both of which date from the early years of this century.

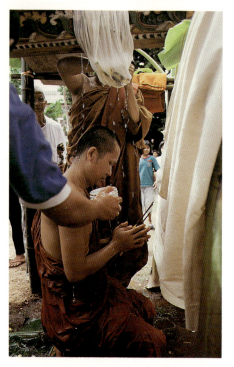

Worth an hour or so of special attention is the public market on Rasada Street, just across from the main terminus for mini-buses. The din is likely to be powerful, and so are some of the smells (particularly during the durian season, the southern variety of this celebrated fruit being rather more potent than those found in Bangkok), but one gets a vivid introduction to the sheer diversity of Thai foodstuffs, ranging from fresh fish to dried spices, as well as to assorted household goods.

A pleasant place to have either lunch or dinner is the restaurant atop Khao Rang, the hill that overlooks the city and offers spectacular views of the harbor and the sea beyond. The area around the restaurant has been landscaped and designated a "Fitness Park" for health enthusiasts; the less athletically inclined are advised to take transportation to the top, however, as it is a considerable climb.

Very few non-Thai visitors choose to stay in town, but Phuket does have several hotels:

On On Hotel Phangonga Road tel. 211154	* 49 fan and air conditioned rooms. With rooms for only Baht 80 the place for a stranded budget traveller to stay in town.
Pearl Hotel Montri Road tel. 211044 Bangkok tel. 2601022–4	** 250 rooms. Phuket Town's first and most popular up-market hotel. Interesting swimming pool with waterfall. Phuket's only massage parlor. Very good penthouse Chinese restaurant.
Phuket Merlin Hotel 158/1 Yaowarat Road tel. 211618, 212866–70	** 180 rooms. The newest luxury hotel in town. Night Club. Popular with businessmen from out of town.

Port of Phuket This is located a short drive east of the town and is used by most of the approximately 350 industrially equipped fishing boats that ply the waters around the island. The scene is colorful, especially around sunrise when the catch is being unloaded and sold to waiting wholesalers, many of whom have refrigerated trucks to carry it all the way to Bangkok. In recent years between 40,000 and 56,000 tons of seafood has been caught annually.

Khao Phra Thaeo National Park Centered on a thickly forested hill, this is one of the last remnants of Phuket's virgin jungle and is

Phuket Town

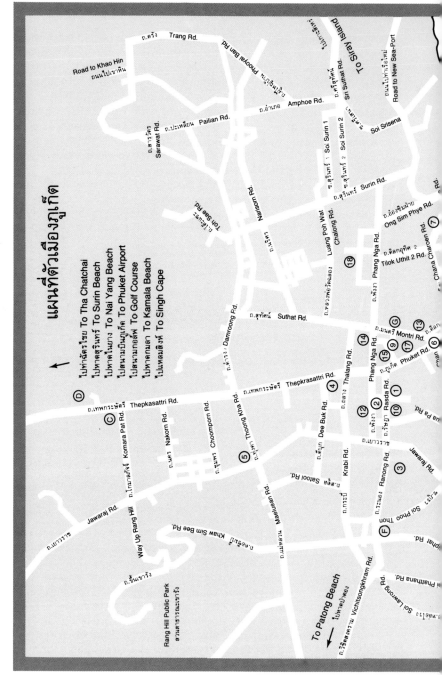

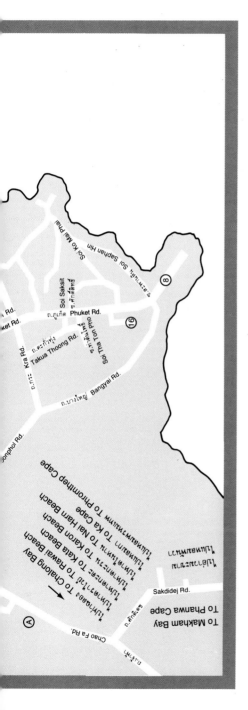

① ธนาคารไทยพาณิชย์ Siam Commercial Bank
② ธนาคารกสิกรไทย Thai Farmers Bank
③ สถานีรถโดยสารภายในจังหวัด Local Bus Station
④ สถานีตำรวจตลาดใหญ่ Talad Yai Police Station
⑤ โรงแรมภูเก็ตเมอร์ลิน Phuket Merlin Hotel
⑥ วงเวียนหอนาฬิกา Clock Tower Circle
⑦ ฟาร์มจระเข้ Crocodile Farm
⑧ อนุสาวรีย์บุกเบิกการทำเหมืองแร่ Mineral Monument
⑨ โรงแรมเพิร์ล Pearl Hotel
⑩ ภูเก็ตคอตติกซาฟารี Phuket Aquatic Safaris
⑪ ภูเก็ตไดเวอร์ Phuket Divers
⑫ On On Hotel
⑬ The Metropole Hotel
⑭ ที่ทำการไปรษณีย์-โทรเลข Post and Telegraph Office
⑮ โทรศัพท์ทางไกลต่างประเทศ Overseas Telephone
⑯ ที่ทำการตรวจคนเข้าเมือง Immigration Office
⑰ ตำรวจท่องเที่ยว T.A.T. = Tourist Authority and Police
⑱ สถานีขนส่งจังหวัดภูเก็ต Phuket Bus Station
⑲ Phuket Mansion
Ⓐ โบสถ์คริสเตียนท่าแครง Takreng Christian Assembly
Ⓑ โบสถ์โรมันคาธอลิค ตลิ่งชัน Talingchan Roman Catholic Church
Ⓒ โบสถ์เซเว่นท์เดย์แอดเวนติส Seventh Day Adventist Church
Ⓓ วัดโฆสิตวิหาร Wat Kosit Viharn
Ⓔ มัสยิดดุลยามียะ ตลิ่งชัน Dylyamiah Mosque Talingchan Road
Ⓕ ศาลเจ้าจุ้ยตุ่ย (ปุ้ดจ้อ) Jui Tui Chinese Temple
Ⓖ Thai International Airways

reached by a road leading from the center of Thalang on the way from the airport. Tone Sai Waterfall, at its best during the rainy season, is popular with day-trippers and can be crowded on weekends but is virtually deserted at other times. The surrounding jungle is magnificent with towering trees, ferns, and exotic palms; among the latter is *Karedoxa dolphin*, a splendid specimen with silvery leaves now found only in Phuket. A restaurant overlooking the waterfall area serves excellent food at reasonable prices. Accommodation is also available here.

Aquarium This is part of the Marine Biological Research Center, overlooking the sea from a picturesque site on Chalong Bay. Open daily, it contains an interesting selection of sea creatures, attractively displayed as well as educational exhibits on methods of fishing. Among the Center's projects is the hatching of eggs laid by the giant sea turtles who come ashore on the island between October and February; the young are reared at the aquarium and later released into the open sea.

Laem Phrom Thep The southernmost tip of Phuket, this prominence is a favored spot from which to view the often spectacular sunsets, as well as several picturesque islands one of which, Koh Kaeo, has a Buddhist *chedi* and meditation cells for monks. Koh Kaeo has a restaurant offering simple food and drink.

Phuket Museum This was opened in early 1987 and is located near the statues of the two local heroines on the road leading in from the aiport. The collection includes old Burmese cannons and other historical relics found in the area.

Wat Chalong This is probably the largest and best-known of Phuket's 29 Buddhist wats, or temples, none as dazzling as the famous ones in Bangkok but nonetheless built in the same fanciful, elaborately decorated style. Enshrined in one of the buildings are statues of two revered 19th century monks, Luang Pho Chaem and Luang Pho Chaung, who helped put down a rebellion by Chinese immigrants in 1876. The images are kept lavishly supplied with offerings of gold leaf, flowers, and lighted incense.

Wat Phra Thong This is another temple worth visiting, located on a road leading north from Thalang on the way to the airport. Its main feature of interest is a large Buddha image, allegedly of gold, half buried in the earth. Legend claims the image was discovered by the father of a child who died after tying his water buffalo to a piece of metal protruding from the ground. Prompted by a dream, the father returned to the spot and dug, managing to excavate only the top part of the statue; Wat Phra Thong was built to shelter the image which in turn was covered with plaster to hide it from invaders.

Lak Muang In most old Thai cities, a shrine was erected at the

"central axis," usually around a wood or stone pillar that marked the center of the settlement and provided a home for the spirit who guarded it. Phuket's pillar is not located in the town itself but near the monument to the two heroines in Tha Rua, once the island's principal community though most traces of it have vanished today. The resident spirit is regarded as a powerful one, capable of granting all sorts of wishes, and the shrine is always full of offerings by local people.

Chinese Temples Of the several Chinese temples on Phuket, the principal ones are at Kathu, where the Vegetarian Festival originated, and Put Jaw Temple in town. Both temples are lavishly adorned with red and gold carvings and images of various gods and goddesses. Because of Phuket's large Chinese-Thai population these temples are rather more crowded than those in other parts of the country.

Sea Gypsy Village Perhaps the most interesting sea gypsy village is on Koh Sire, the large island linked by a bridge to the east of Phuket Town. Normally there is not much going on, but if a visitor is lucky, he might come when the village is celebrating its Loy Rua Festival, at the beginning and end of the fishing season (meaning just before and after the monsoon arrives), when a miniature fishing boat is filled with symbolic offerings and set adrift to propitiate the spirits of the sea. (More detailed information about these tribal people is given on page 104.)

Thai Boxing Bouts are held most Sunday evenings at the boxing stadium at Sapan Hin, on the outskirts of town. Fighters demonstrate the balletic grace and free-for-all techniques that have given this method of self-defence an international renown. A musical accompaniment by a Thai orchestra adds an exotic touch to the proceedings.

Phuket Golf and Country Club Phuket's first 18 hole golf course is located halfway between Phuket Town and Patong Beach near the 6 Kl. marker on that road. Beautifully landscaped, it sits on the site of a former tin mine. Open to the public, course fees run from 500–700 Baht and rental equipment is available at its American run pro-shop. Tel. 213388 for more information.

Yupadeewan Nursery Phuket abounds in beautiful ornamental plants, some of them native and others imported hybrids. Yupadeewan Nursery, the largest on the island, has an impressive selection for sale or just for enjoyment. To reach it, turn left at the Heroine's Monument on the way to the airport and continue for a kilometer or so until you see it on the left.

Muslim Villages Most of the Muslim villages of Phuket have lost the typical atmosphere of their earlier piratical existence, but notwithstanding the modern appearance of the houses today, the

Chinese decorative motifs (top left); Thai decorative motifs ((bottom left, top and bottom right)

A reclining Buddha in the cave temple at Phang Nga (right);
Food stalls line the road approaching this mosque

villagers are still suspicious of outsiders and the villages have a relatively run-down appearance. Traditional houses built without pilings and simply resting on cornerstones can still be seen at Ban Don, Ban Takhian, Ban Naithon (Thalang), Ban Faimai (Phuket) and Phraya Wichitsongkram. The most important mosque on Phuket is Bang Tao Mosque in Chengtalay village near Surin Beach.

The Lak Muang (top left);
Wat Phra Thong (top right)
Wat Chalong (bottom left);
Hermit Cave is a shrine
near Phang Nga on the
mainland (right)

Pansea Beach
(Below) *Detail on a Chinese Temple, Phuket*

From Phuket by Land

By public transportation or hired car an interesting day's trip can be made from Phuket to Phang Nga and Krabi on the mainland, across the Sarasin Bridge.

The road to Phang Nga, 64 kilometers away, passes through scenic views of jungle-covered hills and rubber plantations. Some 12 kilometers before the provincial capital, a track leads to the cave sanctuary called Suwannakuha, noted for its numerous gilded Buddha images, both seated and reclining, as well as for its magnificient limestone formations; many pilgrims come to this impressive sanctuary to make offerings in the form of joss sticks, candles, and flowers.

Just before Phang Nga town is another interesting cave called Tham Russi, or "hermit's cave", located in a public park at the foot of a nearly vertical mountain. This is actually a series of caves, linked by passages; outside the main entrance stands a much-revered statue of a hermit from which the cavern's name derives. Not far away is Khao Chang, "elephant mountain", the silhouette of which is thought to resemble that animal.

Should you wish to spend the night in the Phang Nga area in order to explore the region more thoroughly, there is one luxury accommodation available; **The Phang Nga Bay Resort** at 20 Tha Dan Road. Tel. (076) 411067/70. For reservations from Bangkok Tel. 259-1994/5.

From Phang Nga province, it is also possible to explore the

wonders of Phang Nga and Ao Luk Bays, details of these trips are provided in the following section on trips by boat.

The drive to Krabi, north of Phang Nga, passes through more beautiful jungle scenery distinguished by dramatic limestone hills; Than Bok Koroni National Park, about 45 kilometers before the provincial capital, has a number of waterfalls and trails through the natural forest. Krabi is still relatively untouched by tourism and contains several attractive bays and beaches. For further information on the region around Krabi see page 88.

From Phuket by Boat

From Phuket, there are a number of boat trips one can make to nearby attractions. These have become increasingly popular in recent years, and now tour agencies at all the major beaches can arrange excursions for a variety of prices depending on the number of people and the size of the boat. While the cost of chartering a luxurious junk or yacht may at first seem intimidating, it becomes economical when averaged out between a group of friends. Here are some of the most popular destinations:

Phi Phi Islands

Koh Phi Phi Don and the smaller Koh Phi Phi Le not far away offer breathtaking scenery and tranquil beaches that are still considerably less developed than Phuket. The typical day tour leaves Phuket (usally from Chalong) around eight in the morning and starts back around three thirty, with the journey taking some two hours in good weather (see page 133). Fishing boats can also be hired for a private journey.

Boats generally land at a fishing village on Phi Phi Don, located on a sheltered, curving bay. On one side of the bay, sheer limestone cliffs shaggy with jungle growth rise hundreds of feet out of the translucent sea, while on the other side there are a series of beaches that offer excellent swimming and snorkeling. Simple but adequate bungalows are available near the village for those who want to stay on the island, and several restaurants offer fresh seafood; even simpler (and cheaper) accommodations can be had on some of the beaches for those willing to do without such amenities as a water supply and plumbing.

Thanks to the number of day trippers, the main beach near the village is no longer the best place for swimming, and visitors are advised to head for the beaches on the left, culminating in the one known as Long Beach. By foot the trip can take some time, involving as it does crossing a series of rock formations; it is easiest to take one of the boats near the village pier, at a cost of around ten Baht or so, making sure to arrange return transportation before the scheduled departure for Phuket that afternoon. The water lapping the white sand is incredibly clear, and the coral reefs teem with extraordinary sea-life. Near the tip of the island, the local fishermen stage an impromptu show every morning when they feed leftovers from their catch to sharks; the sharks are not dangerous, however, and there have been no known cases of attack on the island.

Behind the fishing village, there is a lagoon with very shallow water and, at low tide, a wealth of crabs and shellfish which are collected by the local inhabitants.

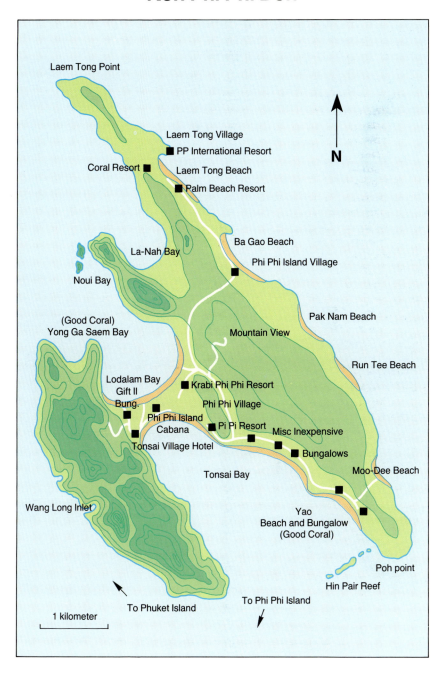

Koh Pi Pi Island is blessed with beautiful, white sandy beaches and surrounded by clear blue sea

Koh Phi Phi Le offers even more dramatic scenery and a number of small, secret coves, each with a snow-white crescent of sand; fewer visitors come here to swim and there is a sense of idyllic escape. One of Phi Phi Le's most celebrated attractions is an immense cave, festooned with theatrical stalactites and stalagmites, where bird's nests are collected and, after processing, dispatched to Chinese gourmets all over the world. Access to the caves is via a rickety bamboo landing — easy enough at high tide with a calm sea but tricky when the water is low or choppy. Visitors are charged an admission fee, as well as forbidden to use flash bulbs inside the cavern since it disturbs the all-important little swifts who build the nests.

The main chamber is as large as a cathedral, rising into inky darkness overhead and filled with the powerful ammoniac smell of guano deposited by countless millions of birds and bats. On one wall are crude but effective paintings of unknown vintage showing various kinds of sailing craft which called at the island to collect the valuable nests in the distant past. At the foot of an impressive stalagmite rising from the floor is an altar regularly supplied with offerings by the Moken or sea gypsies, who do most of the collecting up spindly ladders within the caves.

White birds nests are the most valuable
(Following pages) *Inside a bird's nest cave*

Bird's Nest Soup

How did the Chinese ever acquire a taste for that exotic delicacy known as bird's nest soup? Legend offers several explanations. According to one, a group of sailors were shipwrecked on an island in Southeast Asia and were saved from starvation by the tiny nests. Another legend claims that a eunuch named San Pao was sent by a Ming emperor on an expedition to the Malay archipelago, where he was served nests; impressed by their taste and, even more, by their alleged medicinal powers, he brought some back to his royal patron.

Whatever the origins, the culinary use of bird's nests became a Chinese passion—one much misunderstood in the West, where nests are thought of in terms of twigs, feathers, and other unpalatable ingredients. Actually, as a British naturalist in Sarawak once wrote, "The quality of a bird's nest is as real (as fit a subject for discussion) as the character of a vintage wine to the French wine grower or gourmet," and the nests used are a far cry from the Western conception.

They are produced by a tiny, brown and charcoal colored, forktailed swift known as *Collocalia esculenta*, which favors lofty limestone caves and cliffs as a nesting habitat. The material from which the nests are constructed is a gluey secretion discharged from two glands under the bird's lower jaw; this comes out in long strands that soon dry into a strong, resilient substance after exposure to air. Many of the 76 species

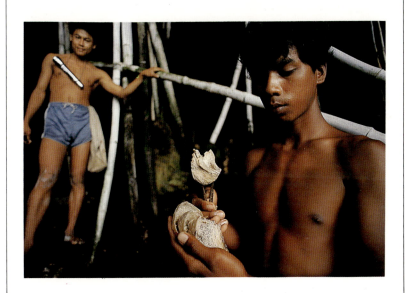

of swifts use this secretion to help weave nests capable of holding up to four chicks, but only two species—the grey–rumped and the brown–rumped swiftlets—build little bracket-like saucers composed entirely of it. These special nests are the ones used in cooking.

The nests, each about four centimetres in diameter, are usually fastened to the upper walls of cliffs and caves, making them difficult to reach. On Koh Phi Phi Le, men climb several hundred feet on spindly bamboo ladders lashed together with fragile-looking raffia to reach them; sticking candles in their caps to light the way, the collectors carry long sticks to pry the nests loose to fall to the floor far below. There have been fatal accidents during this hazardous work, which no doubt explains the altar at the foot of a huge stalagmite in the middle of the cave. A special ceremony is performed during the collection season with offerings of joss sticks, flowers, and little white flags.

In Thailand, as in nearly all other nest-producing countries (among them Malaysia, Indonesia, and the Philippines), the government exercises select control over collection to ensure the bird's survival. A Phuket-based company has exclusive collecting rights and pays the government an annual fee for the privilege. The daredevil climbers climb the ladders three times a year twice between the middle of March and the end of May and then once more in September; after the third harvesting the birds are left undisturbed to raise their young.

Connoisseurs divide the nests into three broad categories: white, red and black. First grade-nests, what the Chinese used to call "bird's nests for officials", are usually obtained only in the first collection and are the purest. The second grade is called "red nest" because it has a reddish tinge, caused not by blood (as is popularly believed) but by twigs eaten by the bird. The lowest grade of all, the so-called "black nest", contains a good deal of foreign matter which has to be carefully removed before the nests can be eaten. Thai nests are graded into more than ten price levels, depending on their purity, with the top bringing around US$100 for 500 grams.

Before going on the market, the nests undergo considerable processing. First they are soaked in water for about half an hour to separate the strands, and after impurities are removed with long tweezers, they are either flattened into sheets or formed into shapes and sulphurated or bleached in the sun. Packed in tins or boxed, nests will keep well for several years.

A famous book on Chinese herbal medicine claims eating the nests "not only strengthens the lungs and accelerates metabolism but also heals coughs and regulates the phlegm." They are also believed to promote virility, delay senility, and cure kidney diseases, upset stomach, measles, and a variety of other ailments. Modern science offers no evidence to support such beliefs, but this has had little effect on their enduring popularity among Chinese gourmets all over the world.

Phang Nga Bay

Unquestionably one of the great scenic attractions of the world is Phang Nga Bay, some 64 kilometers by road from Phuket and about three hours by boat. Visitors to this beauty spot have a choice of either taking one of the regular tour boats from the island or going by car or bus and hiring a boat at Phang Nga itself for the excursion; either option is a full day's trip. There is one good hotel near the bay for visitors who want to explore the many sights in more leisurely fashion.

Millenniums ago, the area was dry land studded with lofty limestone mountains; as glaciers melted, around 10,000 years before the start of the Christian era, the sea invaded to form a bay, leaving only the peaks of the mountains rising from the water in spectacular profusion. The shapes of many are evocative and have resulted in a variety of popular names: Koh Khai (Egg Island), Koh Tapu (Nail Island), Koh Ma Chu (Puppy Island), and Koh Hong (Chamber Island, sometimes called Condo Island because its numerous small caves resemble the rooms in a tall building).

Phang Nga Bay abounds in natural wealth. Its numerous caves yield bird's nests as well as bat guano, much prized as a fertilizer; from its waters come vast quantities of edible jelly fish, much esteemed in Chinese cooking. The dugong, the sea mammal that probably gave rise to the legends of mermaids, is a less common sight than it once was but is still reported from time to time. Groups of dolphins appear and so do such birds as reef egrets, herons, and hornbills. The crab-eating macaque is also still seen. To preserve the area's unique environment, the Thai government has declared it a National Park, the headquarters of which are located near the Phang Nga Bay Resort Hotel.

Though the visitor can see the whole bay in a single tour lasting a few hours, a really thorough exploration involves more time and at least two trips: one through the area nearest the shore as far out as the island of Koh Pannyi and the other of the bay itself. This can be accomplished by spending a night or two at the Bay Resort Hotel and hiring local boats for sightseeing and swimming excursions to some of the islands that have beaches.

A complex network of river estuaries characterizes the shore area, with dense forests of mangrove and nipa palm growing down into the brackish waters. Some of the mangrove trees are raised above the water with aerial roots that support them like stilts, while others have roots that go down and then curve upward and protrude in spokes above the surface. The heavy mangrove wood is used for charcoal manufacture and also for building in local villages. The coast is home to a variety of odd creatures, among them the pigtailed macaque, a proficient swimmer which lives off various sea animals: the fiddler

crab, with one enormous claw and another that looks like an afterthought; and the so-called "walking fish" which can indeed cover considerable distances on land. At a limestone island called Tham Lot, boats are able to pass all the way through a cave which forms a natural arch some 50 meters long, adorned with picturesque stalactites hanging like chandeliers from the roof. Khao Khian, or "Writing Mountain," contains a cave with prehistoric drawings of men and such animals as sharks, crocodiles, and dolphins, believed to have been painted by people who inhabited this region some 3,000 to 4,000 years ago; at one time the sea reached the cave but the sea level has since dropped by about five meters. On the island of Koh Pannyi, at the foot of a towering mountain, is a Muslim fishing village built entirely over the water on stilts; the mountain protects the 2,000-odd villagers from the full force of monsoon storms, but they must go to a neighboring island for their water supply.

Visitors who want to spend a leisurely day on the beach can also take a boat from the hotel to Koh Mak, about an hour's trip. Unlike most of the other islands, this one is not primarily rock but has generous expanses of white sand and coconut palms. There is a small Muslim village here also. A word of caution: if you plan to watch the sunset from Koh Mak, which can be spectacular, be sure to take along a torch as a return to the hotel in total darkness is difficult.

Phang Nga Bay itself is an awesome sight, with literally hundreds of large and small islands rising everywhere in an eerie seascape. Just beyond Koh Pannyi is an island with a lighthouse, where one can land if the waves are not high; from the top the entire bay is spread out in a breathtaking panorama. Boats touring the area often stop at Khao Phingkan, "Leaning Mountain", which has a small beach and an impressive view of Koh Tapu, or Nail island, jutting up from the sea like a huge spike. Khao Phingkan is popularly known today as James Bond Island, since it was used as a setting in the film *The Man With The Golden Gun* (though according to the story it was supposed to be off the coast of China). Tham Kaeo, or "Glass Cave", is reminiscent of Capri's Blue Grotto, with an immense cavern that can be entered by a small boat.

After disembarking, a short walk takes one to a second adjacent cave with a dazzling view of the sea below. Koh Yai Noi and Koh Yai Yai are larger islands in the bay, the latter with a number of fishing villages as well as good beaches.

Worth a separate excursion is a quite separate bay called Ao Luk, east of Phang Nga after passing Koh Mak. The natural scenery is splendid here, with the islands of Koh Chong Lat and Koh Klui being particularly beautiful; both have beaches for swimming. As at Phang

(Below) Elegant palm trees shade these beach bungalows on the island of Koh Phi Phi ; (Right) An aerial of Pannyi village nestling at the foot of a sheer limestone outcrop

Nga, there are numerous smaller limestone outcroppings in weird shapes everywhere one looks.

Koh Pannyi

Koh Pannyi, nestled in the shelter of an immense slab of limestone in Phang Nga Bay, has become a major attraction for tour groups, which stop to enjoy a seafood lunch at one of the numerous restaurants on the island and to photograph the picturesque village on stilts over the water. Despite it quaintness, Koh Pannyi is still a functioning community with a busy life that goes on after the hospitable inhabitants wave farewell to the last of the daily visitors.

Some 400 people make their home in wooden houses resting on sturdy piles of mangrove wood obtained from the nearby coast. Before the advent of tourism the main industry was the production of shrimp paste, which was sold on the mainland; some of the island women still supplement the family income by making this popular ingredient of Thai cuisine. Most families, though, derive a livelihood by catching fish, shrimp, and crabs to supply the restaurants, and even though this market is seasonal — tour boats are rare during the monsoon months — it is enough to sustain the village and even bring such amenities as television and video sets (powered by generators since there is no electricity on the island).

Koh Pannyi boasts a handsome mosque and prayers are broadcast regularly from its minaret. The village has a school with a playground consisting of planks on which the village children enjoy a variety of games. Fresh water must be brought in large drums from a neighboring island to the east. Thanks to the great rock that towers above it, the village is protected from the worst of the monsoon storms, a factor that undoubtedly led to its original siting.

(Below) A rocky overhang, Koh Phi Phi Island
(Right) Navigable sea tunnels pass under the limestone cliffs of Phang Nga Bay

Other islands near Phuket

In addition to the excursions already mentioned, both of which involve a trip of several hours, there are a number of shorter trips that can be made from Phuket to off-shore islands. Boats can be hired through most of the hotels or through agents on the main beaches.

Just east of the tip of Phuket is **Koh Hi**, also known as "Coral Island." In recent years, many of the coral reefs along the coast of Phuket itself have been killed, either through pollution from off-shore tin dredging or dynamiting by fishermen. Those around Koh Hi still flourish, which has made the island popular with snorkelers; there are also several simple but good seafood restaurants along the beach. The nearest main beach from which to reach the island is Rawai, and boats can also be hired at Chalong for a few hours or a full day.

Koh Mai Thong is a little further off-shore and thus takes longer to reach but it has three excellent beaches on the far side and a visitor is unlikely to be disturbed by other swimmers and scuba divers.

Up the eastern coast, just beyond Po Bay, are the islands of **Koh Nakha Yai** and **Koh Nakha Noi**. On the latter is one of Phuket's pearl farms, where oysters are seeded and carefully nurtured over the approximately two years it takes for a pearl to form. Some travel agents in Phuket book tours to the farm for those who want to have the process explained, but those who merely want to enjoy the beach with its views of Phang Nga Bay in the distance can visit on their own. The owner of the farm is currently building some bungalows for visitors who want to spend a night or two on this scenic island.

Lawa Yai Island lies at the southern extremity of the Phang Nga Bay National Park and is popular with day trippers from Phuket.

Pearl Farming

As long ago as the 13th century, it seems, the Chinese had discovered the art of producing cultured pearls through the introduction of foreign bodies into oysters in order to stimulate growth of the coveted nacreous material. It was the Japanese, however, who refined the skill into a profitable industry and one man in particular, Kokichi Mikimoto, who made it world famous. Mikimoto's commercial flair was responsible for the foundation of the company that still bears his name and also for the fact that today cultured pearls are far more common than natural ones.

Cultured pearls are produced in several parts of southern Thailand, including Phuket, often with the advice and financial backing of Japanese companies. In all the operations, the oyster used belongs to the genus *Pinctada*, the same one that produces the best natural pearls, which are mostly collected from the sea by local divers and sold to the company.

In nature, the production of a pearl starts with the accidental intrusion of an alien body into the oyster—a grain of sand, perhaps, or even a small fish or crustacean. The mollusk reacts to this irritant by covering the invader with successive layers of the same material of which its shell is composed, eventually resulting in a solid mass of luminous substance.

High-quality natural pearls have always been rare and greatly prized for their translucent beauty; symbolically, pearls have been seen as the embodiment of such virtues as purity and chastity. Aristocratic Roman ladies wore them while sleeping, according to one writer, so that ". . . their dreams would be filled with lustrous gems," and the Emperor Caligula is supposed to have given a pearl necklace to his favorite horse. Royalty throughout the ancient world vied for the possession of perfect pearls to adorn scepters and crowns as well as the necks of beautiful women.

It was the scarcity of natural pearls as well as their frequently irregular form, that led to the development of cultured pearls and to the foundation of such companies as Naga Pearls, which has farms on Koh Nakha Noi off Phuket and also off Koh Samui in the Gulf of Thailand. The same general method perfected by the Japanese is used. Young *Pinctada* oysters are raised until they are about three years old. At this point they are removed from the water and a technician carefully opens the shell and, using a surgical scalpel, inserts a nucleus stone, a rounded sphere ranging in diameter from about two to eight millimeters. Thus implanted, the oysters are placed in wire baskets and returned to the sea, where they are suspended from rafts or buoys.

If the insertion has been successful, the pearl will begin to develop within a few days. Several layers of the nacreous material are formed each day; in a finished pearl there may be 1,000 or more layers with the formation taking between two and three years for completion. The oysters must be checked periodically, turning them to insure an even coating and moving them up and down to maintain a steady temperature.

Various things can go wrong despite this scientific approach. A misplaced nucleus will result in a poorly shaped pearl (known as a "baroque"), or the oysters may be injured in a monsoon storm or attacked by destructive plankton; on average only about 20 percent will produce pearls of the best quality. The successes, though, compensate for these occasional disappointments: early in 1987, the Naga farm at Koh Samui proudly announced that it had cultured one of the world's largest South Sea pearls. That pearl was "off-round" — meaning not quite spherical in shape — but measured 40 by 33.4 millimeters and weighed an impressive 31 grams.

To get to Koh Nakha Noi (Pearl Island) there are boats leaving regularly from Bang Rong Port which can be reached by following the road tht goes East from the Heroine's Monument.

More Distant Excursions

Similan Islands
For dedicated snorkelers and scuba divers a more ambitious excursion would be one to the Similan Islands northwest of Phuket, which offers spectacular diving opportunities. The Similans consist of eight islands and were officially classified as a national park three years ago. Most visitors have elected to live on hired yachts, making expeditions by small boat to the numerous reefs in the area, but a camp site has been established on Miang Island, the largest of the group and the place where boats generally anchor.

Boats seating between 30 and 40 people can be rented at Rawai Beach on Phuket for the trip to the Similans, at a price of around 5,000 Baht; the journey takes some four hours during the monsoon-free months, November through April. Toilet facilities are available on Miang Island, but there are no bungalows or restaurant facilities; tents sleeping two each, however, can usually be rented through the National Parks Division office at Nai Yang. All diving equipment, plus medical supplies, must be brought along.

Krabi
Krabi is one of southern Thailand's most attractive provinces. East of Phuket, Krabi has an attractive beach and picturesque scenery, though little thus far in the way of tourist accommodations; this may change in the near future, however, as the province is currently being touted as a travel destination by the Thai government.

An express boat service, the *Sea King*, leaves from Makham Bay on Phuket for Krabi on Tuesdays and Thursdays at 8:30 am. The 3½ hour journey costs 400 Baht per person one-way and stops at Phi Phi Island en route. The return trip leaves Krabi at 1 pm on Tuesdays and Thursdays also via Phi Phi Island.

Krabi Hotels:

Krabi Resort
Tambon Ao Nang
tel. 611389, 611915
Bangkok tel. 2518094

**
80 bungalows.

Naowarat Hotel
Uttarakit Road
tel. 611581-2

**
58 rooms.

Wiang Thong
155-7 Uttarakit Road
tel. 611188, 611592-3

*
129 rooms.

Phi Phi Island Hotels (book in Krabi):

Phi Phi Island Cabana
Phi Phi Don Island
tel: (075) 611496 (Krabi)

*
100 rooms and bungalows. Situated on the spectacular Tonsai Beach of Phi Phi Island.

Phi Phi Village
c/o Wiang Thong Hotel (Krabi)

**
Several bungalows.

P P International Resort
Laem Tong Beach
tel. 214272, 214297 (Phuket)

***
Complete facilities except for swimming pool.

Su San Hoi (Shell Cemetery Beach) is located in Ban Laem Pho, some 17 kilometers from town. Petrified shells, some as old as 75 million years, form slabs of rock along the beach. The 'shell cemetery' is exceedingly unusual. The entrance is marked by a nearby Chinese temple.

Paradise, Koh Phi Phi

About 5 kilometers from Su San Hoi is the long white shady beach of **Ao Phra Nang**. A small cave bearing the same name is nearby.

Hat Noppharat Thara, about 2 kilometers from Ao Phra Nang, is a scenic beach lined with casuarina trees which extend for several kilometers. A rocky island about one kilometer from the mainland can be reached by foot at low tide. Mini-buses run regularly from Krabi market to Hat Noppharat. The fare is approximately 20 Baht.

Khanab Num Mount can be reached by hiring a boat from the pier in Krabi. The mount has a cave beautifully decorated with stalactites and stalagmites.

There are various caves worth visiting along Highway No.4 (the route to Ao Luk). These include:

Sua Cave, about 3 kilometers from the Provincial Scout Camp, houses the meditation spot of Wat Tham Sua (Tiger Cave Monastery). The small cave of **Tham Sadet** lies 1 kilometer from km marker 113 off Highway No.4. **Tham Lot** and **Tham Phi Hua To** are unspoiled caves which can be reached by 15-minute boat ride from Tao Than village in Amphoe Ao Luk. Some 45 kilometers from town there is a natural reservoir, **Than Bok Khoran** supporting hundreds of birds. The peaceful atmosphere is ideal for relaxation, picnics and swimming.

A typical Thai country temple

Tarutao National Park
Finally, a rather more distant goal for a voyage along the Thai coast is Tarutao National Park, comprised of 51 mountainous islands in the Andaman Sea near Malaysia. The most beautiful of the islands is **Adang**, which has superb beaches and coral reefs, though many of the others also have attractions of their own. There are some simple accommodations at the park headquarters and on Adang and **Tarutao**.

The beaches in this region have become the latest "traveller's paradise" and will amost certainly soon became mainstream tourist meccas. Try and see them now while they are still in a pristine state.

Rubber trees are tapped during early dawn hours;
(Following page) A rubber plantation

Cultivated Plants of Phuket

Despite the incursions of tin miners and the current construction boom, Phuket still impresses the newcomer with its lush tropical greenery. Only a small percentage of the land area, 7.2 percent to be exact, represents the dense jungle that once dominated the landscape, and most of that lies in the protected Khao Phra Thaeo National Park. The remainder of Phuket's vegetation consists of gardens, fields, and orchards that contribute to Phuket's economy as well as to its scenic allure. Among the more common cash crops are the following:

Rubber
Asia's first seedlings of *Hevea brasiliensis* (known to the world as 'rubber'), arrived at Singapore Botanical Gardens in 1877, having been germinated in England at Kew Gardens from Brazilian seeds. Contrary to legend, they were not stolen from their homeland; the Brazilian government co-operated fully in their export, perhaps to its later chagrin. Only 11 seedlings survived to be planted in the gardens; from these Henry Nicholas Ridley, the Director, later devised a way to propagate them rapidly and tap them for their lucrative white sap. The first person to gamble on growing *Hevea* commercially was a Chinese tapioca planter in Malacca in 1896; his bold step irrevocably changed the economic future of Malaysia.

Uniform isles of mature rubber trees

Phuket soon profited as well. The first rubber trees on the island appeared in 1903 and steadily expanded to the point where plantations now dominate agricultural land and produce an estimated 14,000 tons of dry latex annually. There are a few large estates but most are small groves owned by individual farmers who bring their rubber to a central plant for processing.

Young rubber trees are generally obtained from a government agriculture station on the island, which has developed clones that give a better yield than older varieties. It takes about seven years before the trees can be profitably tapped, and during this long period most growers derive a livelihood by intercropping; (pineapples, which produce exceptionally sweet fruit twice a year, are the current favorite, followed by tapioca and seasonal market vegetables.) Tapping rubber still follows the method pioneered by Ridley a century ago: making a slanted incision in the trunk of the tree in the early hours of the morning and hanging a cup to collect the sticky white sap. Some seven hours later, in the afternoon, the cups are emptied into large trays to stiffen into latex.

Coconuts

Unlike rubber, the coconut is indigenous to Phuket and both large and small of these graceful palms are ubiquitous. Aside from those in private gardens and those growing more or less untended, there are about 5,000 hectares of planted coconuts on the island, yielding some 30 million nuts a year. Every part of the palm is utilized for some purpose: the fronds for thatching roofs, the trunks for sturdy posts in building, the nuts themselves for copra, oil, fiber, or their sweet liquid and succulent meat. Despite this abundance of nuts, however, coconut milk is not a common ingredient in southern Thai food, as it is elsewhere in the country, and more coconuts go into copra production.

Pineapples

Like the chili pepper, the pineapple is a native of tropical America and probably came to Asia with the Portuguese in the 16th century. Both plants spread so widely and successfully that many people mistakenly assume they are indigenous species. The pineapple has a short, stiff stem and shallow roots specially adapted for holding moisture and is thus ideally suited for sandy soil near the sea. In recent years Thailand has led the world in pineapple production, growing some 1.65 million tons around the country. Pineapples are often intercropped with rubber tree seedlings. It takes over a year for a plant to produce a spike of blue-violet blossoms which in turn develops into a pineapple; though this appears to be a single fruit, it is in fact a cluster of 100 or more fruitlets, one from each blossom on the spike. Only one fruit is harvested from a plant, after which it is cut off and a ratoon, or shoot, is allowed to grow for a second crop. By staggering planting times, Phuket produces pineapples almost all year around.

Cashews

These are a few cashew nut orchards on Phuket, but most of these attractive, glossy-leafed trees are grown individually or in small groves in private compounds. Anyone who sees one bearing will understand why the nuts are so expensive, since each tennis-ball sized fruit yields exactly one cashew.

Miscellaneous Fruits

Thailand is justly famous for its high-quality fruits, both seasonal and year-round. Perhaps the most celebrated example of seasonal fruits is the durian, a large and spiny, grey-green fruit which during the hot season permeates local markets with its distinctive odor. In central Thailand, growers have developed hybrids which are so delicate in flavor and aroma that they sometimes seduce even confirmed durian-haters. But southerners generally still prefer the older varieties, which smell to high heaven and have an assertive durian taste, especially when eaten at room temperature. (The durian, incidentally, may be the only fruit in the world to have figured in a penal code; an ancient Thai law classified it as an offensive weapon and prescribed a penalty based on the number of puncture wounds a victim suffered from its sharp spines.)

Mangoes, another hot season fruit, enjoy more widespread popularity. Thai varieties are very different from those found in most other countries, with a far more subtle meat ranging from pale to dark yellow in color. Some are eaten ripe, often accompanied by a side dish of glutinous rice ("sticky rice") sweetened with coconut milk, but Thais also have a passion for green mangoes made into salad (yam) or eaten as a snack with salt.

Resembling the durian in appearance but with a taste of its own, the jackfruit grows from the trunk of the bearing tree. In the South, jackfruit are known as *champada* and often turn up among dessert fruits, as well as an ingredient of curries.

Bananas, like coconuts, are an essential part of the tropical landscape and grow so widely in Phuket that they have escaped local gardens and now grow wild in the forest. The most popular local variety produces fragrant, finger-sized fruit which are boiled in coconut milk as a sweet.

Papaya, or *malakaw*, is a year-round favorite, and nearly every compound boasts one or two to provide for family consumption. Papaya reproduces bisexually; the male plants are distinguished by long sprays of pale green, scented flowers and the females by the heavy fruit growing from near the top of the trunk.

Bright pink rose apples (*chompoo*), deep-purple mangosteens (*mangkut*), and prickly red rambutans (*ngo*) also turn up in many Phuket gardens, though they are not grown commercially on the island; guavas (*farang*) appear regularly as well, the fruit always being eaten green (with salt and pepper) or pickled since Thais do not like them ripe.

Visitors may notice a tall tree with feathery leaves, rather resembling the familiar Flame of the Forest. These trees are called *sato* and produce a long, bean-like fruit that figures prominently in many southern dishes; the sharp, bitter taste does not appeal to everyone but is undeniably one of the characteristic flavors of Phuket.

Culinary Plants
No Thai house, even the simplest, would be complete without a garden patch or least a few pots devoted to some of the more common herbs used in everyday cooking. There will almost certainly be some clumps of grey-green lemon grass (*takrai*), which leaves a citrus-like tang to many soups; one or more of varieties of sweet basil (*bai kaprow* or *bai horapha*); ginger (*khing*); and the essential chili pepper (*prik*), which come in a dozen or so different sizes and degrees of pungency.

A Chinese-style door found in the Songkla Museum

Eating Thai (with a southern accent)

A wag once described Thai food as coming in three varieties: hot, hotter, and hottest. That sort of generalization should, of course, be taken with a drop of fish sauce. In fact, as numerous visitors have already discovered at Thai restaurants back home (Los Angeles alone has around 300), the country's cuisine is infinitely subtle in its gradations of flavor, which include not only searing chili-hot but also sweet, sour, and salty. An extraordinary range of spices is employed, among them ginger, lemon grass, cardamom, cumin, mace, pepper, garlic, mint, basil, coriander, pandanus, kaffir lime, and more than a dozen kinds of chili peppers. Each part of the country prides itself on distinctive regional dishes.

Southern Thai food has a reputation for being among the hottest. Malay-style dishes, reflecting Indian influences in their use of turmeric and curry powder, are common, and so is a fondness for a large variety of vegetable and fruit condiments; coconut milk, popular in central Thai cooking, is rarely used. A staple of the region is *gang mussaman*, a thick curry of either beef chicken cooked with potatoes, mixed herbs, and peanuts. Seafood, naturally, predominates—even the least imposing establishment will offer fresh fish, crabs, and prawns, and sometimes lobsters as well, though Thais have developed a liking for the latter only in comparatively recent years.

Soups in the south are particularly spicy; be wary of the tiny green chillies, the most pungent of all, which are employed with a lavish abundance. Another distinctive southern touch is the use of several extremely bitter vegetables, among them a bean called *sato*; these are very definitely an acquired taste, but they are undoubtedly what residents of the region miss most when they move elsewhere in the country.

A Thai meal is an informal affair with no prescribed sequence of courses. The centerpiece is invariably a large tureen of rice surrounded by other dishes—usually some kind of curry, a soup, a grilled or steamed fish, and a salad or vegetable—to be eaten in any order or combination. Fish sauce (*nam pla*), both plain and mixed with chillies, as well as sugar and ground chillies, are always available to help adjust the flavors. Dessert generally consists of fresh fruits; Phuket's pineapples, harvested all year round, are famous for their juicy sweetness, and during the hot season such delicacies as mango and durian make a much-awaited appearance on the market.

Some recommended Phuket delicacies:
Kanom Chin: Thai rice noodles eaten with curry soup. Although available everywhere in Thailand, the Phuket variety has a richer flavor when taken with a beef or crab curry and local fresh vegetables.

Mee Hokkian: Literally 'Hokkian Noodles' referring to the southern Chinese province are delicious when fried with fresh shrimps, pork, shellfish and green cabbage.

Ho Mok: A curried fish or crab dish steamed with vegetables in a banana 'cup' usually eaten with plain rice. Ho Mok is noted for its pungent flavor.

Namphrik Kung Siap: This is Phuket's version of a spicy shrimp paste sauce common throughout Thailand. Resembling a dip, the namphrik is eaten with crisped shrimps and raw vegetables.

Sea Gypsies

The oldest, and probably the most exotic, inhabitants of Phuket are the tribal people usually referred to by Europeans as sea gypsies. The Thais call them *Chao Nam*, "water people", or sometimes *Chao Thalay*, "sea people."

Actually both names are somewhat misleading since they tend to lump together what are in fact three separate groups: the Moken, the Moklen, and the Urak Lawoi. The Moken, sea faring nomads, are the only ones with true gypsy characteristics, spending most of their lives in boats and coming ashore mainly during the monsoon for temporary residence. The Moklen and the Urak Lawoi live in more or less permanent seaside villages, and while they have not yet been totally absorbed into the Thai community they have still lost much of their cultural distinction. The confusion between the three groups is understandable since there has been considerable intermarriage, particularly between the Moklen and the Urak Lawoi, and all three groups are frequently found living in the same villages today.

For centuries these peoples have existed along the coast from southern Burma to Malaysia. Many historians identify the Moken with the buccaneering Saleiters who terrorized 17th-century voyagers and supposedly helped the first ruler of Malacca establish his kingdom (for which service they were rewarded with hereditary titles of nobility). Not everyone, however, accepts this identification. David W. Hogan, who wrote a monograph on the groups, notes the singularly un-warlike quality of all three tribes today and comments, "Possibly in a former century they may have been enlisted by others to man piratical boats but it is hard to imagine them as instigating such raids themselves."

Today all three groups share several general characteristics. They tend to be timid and many show a distrust of modern civilization, regarding it, in Hogan's words, "as a hostile environment with which they cannot cope." Most suffer from a sense of inferiority and resent such names as Chao Nam and Chao Thalay, though those who have become Thai citizens are proud to be called Thai Mai, or "New Thai".

The sea is their real element. Even the Urak Lawoi, who often take inland jobs with tin-mining companies, insist on making their home near the water, saying they cannot sleep unless they can hear the sound of waves. All are superb swimmers, able to stay in the water for hours at a time and able to work at great depths. They are the source of nearly all the shells and coral in Phuket shops, as well as many of the rarer shellfish offered in restaurants. On land they seem singularly unaffected by vertigo and are willing to climb rickety bamboo ladders to harvest edible birds' nests from the heights of caves on off-shore islands.

Each tribal village is guarded by a communal spirit house, to which offerings are made, and the spirits of the sea are regularly placated before setting out on fishing or diving expeditions. The main village festivals, each lasting two or three days, are held twice a year during the 6th and 11th lunar months. During these celebrations an elaborate boat is fashioned

from palm leaves, into which are placed wooden dolls representing the members of each household; other offerings may include chili peppers, cakes, fish paste, hair clippings and finger-nail parings, as well as puffed rice which children have rubbed over their bodies. On the 14th day of the lunar month, the boat is released at sea, taking with it the bad luck of the villagers, who celebrate this cleansing with a gala party.

There are three tribal villages on Phuket today. The largest and most prosperous is at Koh Sire, near the port, which has well-constructed houses and a school; many of the men work for mining companies or on fishing boats, though some families collect shells for local shops. The oldest village is at the north end of Rawai Beach; this is much poorer than the Koh Sire settlement, particularly the part inhabited by Moken, who earn their living mainly from selling fish and shells to Phuket agents. The poorest of all is at Sepum, some seven kilometers north of Phuket Town, where the income mostly comes from gathering shellfish and making nipa-palm thatching.

Festivals and Holidays

Phuket celebrates most of Thailand's major festivals and holidays as well as one, the Vegetarian Festival, that is all its own. The dates of several are determined by the lunar calendar, which means they may vary by a week or so each year, but the following will serve as a general month-by-month guide:

January
Both New Year's Eve and January 1 are official holidays, with the same noisy midnight festivities found over most of the world. All the large hotels and bungalow complexes arrange some celebration for their guests; one of the most spectacular fireworks displays is that staged by the Club Med, which can be enjoyed from Kata Beach by non-guests as well.

February
Makha Bucha, an important Buddhist holiday commemorating the miraculous occasion when 1,250 disciples gathered spontaneously to hear the Buddha preach, usually falls toward the end of the month, depending on the moon. During the day the local temples are crowded with people making merit by offering food to the monks and releasing caged birds. In the evening there is a candlelit procession around the main building of the temple complex.

Chinese New Year also falls during this month. In Phuket (with its large Chinese population) this is an occasion for more sustained festivities than elsewhere in Thailand, though it is not a national holiday. There are ceremonies at the important Chinese temples such as Kathu and Jui Tui, and there are family gatherings at home; many local shops and businesses are likely to close for several days. Resorts are crowded with visitors from Singapore, Malaysia, and Hong Kong.

April
Chakri Day, a national holiday celebrated on April 6, commemorates the founding of the Chakri Dynasty which still occupies the Thai throne, the present King being the ninth ruler. Government offices and many shops are elaborately decorated for the occasion.

Songkran, the traditional Thai New Year celebration, takes place between the 13th and 15th, though only one day is an official holiday. Songkran is in part a religious occasion, and many people go to the temples in the morning to make merit. Foreign visitors, however, are more likely to notice the exuberant merrymaking that takes place in the streets, characterized by throwing liberal quantities of water on any

passersby. High spirits prevail, and a thorough soaking can be refreshing in Thailand's hottest month.

May
Coronation Day, on the 5th, is a national holiday marking the anniversary of the coronation of King Bhumibol Adulyadej.
Visaka Bucha, also a national holiday, is the most important Buddhist event of the year and usually falls during May. It celebrates the birth, death, and enlightenment of the Buddha; in the evening there are candlelit processions at nearly all the island's temples.

July
Asalha Bucha, marking the Buddha's first sermon to his first five disciples, is immediately followed by Khao Phansa, the beginning of Buddhist Lent; both are national holidays. Many young men choose the three month observance of Lent to go into the priesthood, and ordination ceremonies are common just before Lent commences.

August
Her Majesty Queen Sirikit's Birthday falls on the 12th of this month and is observed as a national holiday.

October
Og Phansa marks the end of Buddhist Lent and also the end of the rainy season in most parts of Thailand, though not necessarily in Phuket. This is the season for *Kathins*, when groups organize merit-making processions to present robes and other offerings to Buddhist monks throughout the country.
Chulalongkron Day, on the 23rd, commemorates the day on which this beloved king died.
The ten-day Vegetarian Festival, Phuket's biggest annual celebration, also falls during October. (See page 112)

November
Loy Krathong, one of Thailand's loveliest festivals, usually comes in the early part of this month, though it sometimes falls towards the end of October. Under the light of the full moon, crowds of people launch little lotus-shaped boats called *krathongs* on every available body of water, including the sea. Each *krathong* is adorned with a lighted candle, incense sticks, and floral offerings. The ceremony honors the water spirits and, so some believe, the *krathongs* carry away the bad luck of those who launch them. Phuket's observance is not as spectacular as those of Bangkok or Chiang Mai, but the atmosphere can be charming and the mood festive.

Celebrating the Vegetarian Festival

December

The birthday of His Majesty King Bhumibol Adulyadej is celebrated on December 5; this is a national holiday.
Constitution Day, on December 10, commemorates Thailand's first constitution.

Vegetarian Festival

Basically Chinese in origin and practice, Phuket's Vegetarian Festival has assimilated elements from other cultures over the years and is now a unique combination of religious piety, ritual, merry-making, and spectacular displays of supernatural powers.

The festival's origins are obscure, but it appears to have started in the mid-19th century in the centrally-located Khatu District among Chinese who flocked to work as tin miners. Many of these immigrants were undoubtedly familiar with the ancient Chinese practice of turning vegetarian for a period of time, generally during the ninth month of the lunar calendar. Abstaining from meat was supposed to purify the body and mind, avert potential disaster, and generally promote good fortune.

Despite knowledge of the tradition, however, the idea of staging a local festival did not evolve until a series of events took place at a settlement called Baan Katun, which was established in the Khatu District around 1825. In those days, the area was not the most salubrious part of Phuket, being covered with dense forests teeming with dangerous animals and deadly fevers that felled the workers in large numbers. Nevertheless, with tin prices rising, Khatu attracted increasing numbers of immigrants to work the mines, as well as others eager to cash in on the boom-town atmosphere.

Among the camp-followers was a touring Chinese opera company. Business was so good the troupe stayed for almost a year, putting on nightly shows for the homesick miners, before disaster struck: the entire cast came down with fever, along with a sizeable part of the local population.

It was then that several of the actors recalled the vegetarian rites and began to wonder if their misfortunes might not proceed from their failure to observe them, as they had faithfully done back in their native country. Accordingly, they performed a makeshift version of the ceremony at their theater. It was not complete, they told the miners who joined in; they lacked some of the necessary ritual objects as well as an expert to guide them. But, all the same, their impromptu effort proved dramatically effective. The troupe and many of the local people recovered quickly, making such an impression that a shrine was erected — about 50 meters from the present-day Khatu Temple — and it was decided to continue the practice every year.

There remained, however, a nagging sense of incompleteness; and one of the workers, who claimed to be familiar with the rites, told his compatriots that an important item they lacked was a proper ceremonial vessel in which to place the burning incense sticks. He offered to fetch one from Kungsai, his birthplace in China, if they would raise the funds to send him. The Khatu people decided it was in their interests to do so and the man departed, promising to return soon.

When two or three years passed without word, many in the village began to suspect they had been the victims of a confidence trick. But then one day a message arrived: the man had indeed come back and wanted the people to come take possession of the vessel at a place then called Baan Niew — today known as Sapan Hin, or Stone Bridge — near the beach where his ship had landed.

A grand procession formed to receive the sacred object and bear it triumphantly back to the Khatu Temple. The man also brought a number of scripture books, explaining in detail how to conduct the ceremony, and these are still kept at the shrine.

Phuket now has five important Chinese temples, and all of them observe the Vegetarian Festival, starting on the first day of the ninth lunar month, usually in October. The biggest celebration is held at Jui Tui Temple on Ranong Road in town, followed by that at Bang Neow Temple, also in town, and at the original site of Khatu Temple. Some of the rites at the different temples overlap, but an effort is made to stagger them so that everyone can enjoy all the various processions and performances.

A thorough cleaning of the shrines takes place on the day before the ceremony begins. Sandalwood and joss sticks are burned to purify the precincts. In the afternoon, a large post is erected before each shrine to serve as a residence for the nine spirits who preside over the rites; their presence is symbolized by nine lamps hung on the post.

The gods are honored with vegetarian food offerings which are essentially the same as the diet observed by believers during the festival period: rice, cabbage, beans, carrots, pumpkins, and various fruits. People may eat this food at the temples or take it home; all the raw materials have been donated in advance by the community.

Each temple displays a formidable array of knives, swords, axes, and other weapons which play a prominent role in the ceremony as it is presently observed on Phuket. It is believed that the supernatural powers of the gods are transferred to those who have purified themselves, thus enabling believers to endure a wide variety of self-inflicted ordeals, from forcing sharp rods through their cheeks to walking on red-hot coals, without pain either during or after. There is no record of such practices being part of the Vegetarian Festival in ancient China, and very likely they were borrowed from India, where self-mortification is frequently found in Hindu ritual.

Another integral part of all observances is the Bridge Crossing Ceremony, which alleviates bad fortune. The participants believe these rites will not only relieve present difficulties but also mitigate those which may lie in the future.

Finally, each temple stages a fire-walking and knife-blade climbing extravaganza. To outsiders, these seem nothing short of miraculous, defying all physical laws, for the purified do indeed walk calmly over beds of glowing charcoal and scale ladders with rungs of razor-sharp blades. To disprove trickery, viewers are welcome to try themselves — though the lack of volunteers is conspicuous.

On the final evening everyone gathers in the city for a grand bash, complete with non-stop firecrackers to chase away bad spirits and accompany the nine gods on their annual journey back to heaven. At midnight the last rites are performed, the explosions subside, and Phuket returns to normal for another year. The dates of the festival fall between October 17–26 in 1990.

Turtle Release Festival There are five different species of giant turtles inhabiting the Andaman Sea and western shores of Phuket. The largest of these, the Leatherback, weighs as much as 850 kilos and can be more than 2 meters (7 feet) in length. Every winter (October through February), the Leatherbacks emerge from the sea to lay their eggs in holes they have dug in the sand of Nai Yang and Mai Kao beaches. Once a common sight, the popularity of the turtle eggs as yet another Asian delicacy, has reduced their numbers so radically that the turtles are now considered a protected and rare species. The Marine Biological Research Centre of Phuket began raising the turtles in captivity with the aim of releasing them into the natural environment and thus hopefully replenishing their dwindling numbers. Since 1979, it was stipulated that the young turtles were to be released into the ocean every year on April 13 off Nai Yang Beach not far from the airport, a date which corresponds with Songkran Day (see page 107). On this day special activities precede the release of the turtles, usually around 6 pm, such as sporting events and cook-outs.

A Poet on Phuket

Aside from appearing in various historical accounts, Phuket has inspired at least one poet to extol its charms. Around 1839, a certain Nai Mi spent over a year on the island and later wrote an imaginative account that at times strains the limits of poetic license but is nonetheless wonderfully vivid.

Nai Mi was a favorite pupil of Sunthorn Phu, regarded as the greatest Thai poet of the Bangkok period. Nai Mi was ordained as a monk during the third reign (1824–1851) and it was in this capacity that he made what was then an epic journey — by ship, paddle boat, foot, and elephant — to the south, accompanied by a group of friends.

Despite his priestly robes, Nai Mi had an observant eye for such mundane matters as commerce and other secular concerns. Here are some of his comments on life in Phuket Town:

"The merchant shops and bazaars on shore hustle and encroach upon one another. Tin is bartered for dollars, commodities are hawked all around. Siamese, Chinese, Malay, Javanese (mostly from Sumatra) piece goods retailers heap up flowered chintzes in piles or in long rows; some sell colored silk fabrics of different kinds."

And on local women:

"Handsomely built damsels are in evidence; but awe-struck, I dare not glance upon them. For I am deeply afraid of their subtle philtres and craftily concocted charms that so easily lead to perdition. I prefer to refrain from all intercourse or meddling with them, as I think this would bring shame upon myself . . . The youngsters from the central provinces that I have brought along with me managed to get on far better with them, with whom some of them became attached . . . (The) women are, in fact, exceedingly clever talkers: they excel in the art of charming the ear and netting partners. Once they make love to a lad, it is done with him; he is inextricably inveigled."

And for a glimpse of how he exercised his poetic imagination, here is an account of a stroll, probably along Chalong Bay:

"Beyond the village I came upon the seashore, and walked along the beach over the sand banks. I contemplated meanwhile the majestic expanse: it was deep and merrily noisy, with its foaming surges relentlessly breaking on the shore, so vehemently as to cause the sandbanks, the rocks, and the land all around to quake. I listened to the mighty roar of the surf which made my heart shudder with awe. The ocean stretches before the view boundless and fathomless, and teems with aquatic animals of all kinds . . . Crocodiles, Heras [a web-footed water lizard] spring up side by side in flocks out of the billows. Water snakes and mermaids dart forth, in a swinging zig-zag gait, to disport themselves with their mates or swim past in close pairs of unbroken procession. Crabs, shrimps, prawns, and dragons wander about wagging their tails among the waves."

Index to Useful Information

Travel information
  Air   119
  Bus   122
  Local   122
  Boats and Auto Rental   124

Useful Addresses and Phone Numbers
  Important numbers   126
  Banks   126
  Hospitals and Clinics   127
  Restaurants   128
  Night entertainment   132
  Places of Worship   133
  Shopping   133

Travel Information

Air Transport

Domestic

The national air carrier, *Thai Airways International*, flies between Bangkok and Phuket about ten times daily. The flight is one hour and ten minutes long and costs 1,810 Baht one way. The following table illustrates the Bangkok-Phuket-Bangkok daily flight schedules as they stood Sept. 1990. The schedule is likely to change for the winter high season in Oct. 1990 so passengers should confirm their reservations well in advance. Flight delays are frequent—be sure to call before heading off to the airport: in Bangkok call 535-2081/2 and Phuket call 311175. Unfortunately, Thai's services have recently sunk to abysmal new lows—they simply can not cope with the explosive growth in travel within the country.

Bangkok–Phuket Scheduled Flights

Bangkok-Phuket

Mondays
 7.45, 9.45, 11.30, 12.00, 13.30, 14.30, 16.00, 17.45, 19.15

Tuesdays
 7.45, 7.50, 9.45, 11.30, 12.00, 13.00, 14.30, 16.00, 17.45, 19.15

Wednesdays
 7.45, 9.45, 11.30, 12.00, 13.30, 14.30, 16.00, 17.45, 19.15

Thursdays
 7.45, 7.50, 9.45, 11.30, 12.00, 13.00, 14.30, 16.00, 17.45, 19.15

Fridays
 7.45, 8.30, 9.45, 11.30, 12.00, 13.30, 14.30, 16.00, 17.45, 19.15

Saturdays
 7.45, 7.50, 9.45, 11.30, 12.00, 14.30, 16.00, 17.45, 19.15

Phuket-Bangkok

8.00, 8.40, 9.45, 13.30, 16.50, 17.35, 18.00, 20.15

8.00, 8.40, 9.45, 10.30, 13.30, 16.50, 18.00, 19.00, 19.15, 20.15

8.00, 8.40, 9.45, 13.30, 16.50, 17.35, 18.00, 19.00, 20.15

8.00, 8.40, 9.45, 13.30, 16.50, 18.00, 19.15, 20.15

8.00, 8.40, 9.45, 13.30, 16.50, 19.00, 20.15

8.00, 8.40, 9.45, 10.30, 13.30, 16.50, 17.35, 18.00, 20.15

Sundays
7.45, 8.30, 9.45, 11.30, 12.00,   8.00, 8.40, 9.45, 13.30, 16.50,
13.30, 14.30, 16.00, 17.45,   18.00, 19.00, 20.15
19.15

Thai Airways International also operates a fleet of smaller aircraft that service other destinations in Thailand from Phuket. The one-way fares and flight frequencies are as follows:

Phuket—Hat Yai	45 min. or 1 hr. 5 min.	675 Baht 3 times daily
Phuket—Surat Thani	30 min. or 45 min.	385 Baht 2 times daily
Phuket—Nakhon Si Thammarat	45 min.	575 Baht daily
Phuket—Trang	45 min.	330 Baht 2, 4, 5, 6, 7
Phuket—Chiang Mai	2 hr. 10 min.	2,805 Baht 1, 3, 4

In addition, **Bangkok Airways** flies to/from Koh Samui daily. The flight is 40 min. and costs 1,000 Baht one way.

International Flights

There are direct, scheduled international flights to Phuket from Hong Kong, Singapore, Kuala Lumpur, Penang, Langkawi Island (Malaysia), Frankfurt, Vienna, Sydney, Copenhagen, Stockholm and Amsterdam with charter flights from Switzerland, the UK and Germany scheduled to begin service in 1991. **Dragon Air** flies daily except Friday between Hong Kong and Phuket, the fare is 7,730 Baht one way, although an excursion ticket good for 3–7 days costs only 9,685 Baht round trip. The trip lasts 3 hr. and 20 min. In Phuket call 215734 for schedule and reservations. **Tradewinds** connects Singapore to Phuket daily for 3,965 Baht one way or buy an excursion fare for 4,805 Baht round trip if you stay in Singapore for 2–14 nights. The flight takes 1 hr. and 40 min. In Phuket call 213891–5 or in Singapore 2212221. Three destinations in Malaysia are connected to Phuket by direct flights. The following chart outlines these services:

Phuket—Penang	Mon–Sat 50 min.	Thai 1,285 Baht
Phuket—Kuala Lumpur	Tues, Wed, Thurs, Sun 1 hr. 10 min.	Thai 2,150 Baht
	Wed, Fri, Sun 1 hr. 10 min.	Malaysian 2,315 Baht
Phuket—Langkawi Island	Fri 40 min.	Malaysian 975 Baht

Lauda Air flies to Phuket twice weekly from Vienna. The flight is about 8 hours long and depart Saturdays from Vienna arriving 3 a.m. in Phuket and then continue on to Sydney, Australia. The aircraft stops in Phuket again on its way back to Vienna from Sydney. **Condor**, a German airline based in Frankfurt, flies from that city to Phuket every Saturday, arriving Phuket at 18:00 and returning to Frankfurt that same evening at 19:00. **Stirling Air** of Denmark connects Phuket to Copenhagen twice a week and also flies a Boeing 757 from Stockholm to Phuket weekly. **Martin Air** flies weekly from Amsterdam to Phuket using an Airbus A-300. Charter licenses are held by **Australian Airlines**, **Caledonian** of Great Britain and **LTU** of Germany, all of whom fly charter groups to Phuket from Europe and Australia.

Thai Airways provides a limousine service to the airport from its office at 78 Ranong Road in Phuket Town for 50 Baht per passenger. Tel. 216776 for more information. The airport departure tax is 150 Baht for international flights and 20 Baht for domestic routes. For the really down and out a local bus connects Phuket Town to the airport from the market on Ranong Road between 9 and 11 a.m. only. The 15 mile journey lasts at least one hour. Private taxi fares to the airport cost around 200 Baht from Phuket Town up to 350 Baht from the southern beach locations. A tuk-tuk can be chartered for 150 Baht from Town to the airport and can carry about six people with their luggage.

Trains

There is no rail service to Phuket. The nearest station is at Surat Thani from which buses may be taken to Phuket, a trip of some six to eight hours over winding mountain roads and costing around 180 Baht.

Buses

There are several companies operating air conditioned bus service between Phuket and Bangkok. This trip takes at least 14 hours and can be arduous due to the limited leg room. The fare is 300 Baht one-way. For the real masochist there are non-airconditioned government run buses leaving daily from Phuket Town's Phang Nga Rd. bus terminal at 8.25 am, 10.55 am, 12.35 pm, 2.15 pm, 3.20 pm, 4.20 pm, and 6.30 pm. One-way fare is 165 Baht. The following companies may be contacted for ticket reservations:

Transportation Comp.	Tel.	211480
Phuket Tour		212892
Yarnyont Tour		211533
Phuchong Tour		211662

Other destinations serviced by non-airconditioned buses from Phuket are as follows:

Phuket-Hat Yai	8 hr.	91 Baht (154 Baht air)
Phuket-Trang	6 hr.	62 Baht
Phuket-Surat Thani	6 hr.	61 Baht (150 Baht air)
Phuket-Nakhon Si Thammarat	8 hr.	76 Baht
Phuket-Krabi	4 hr.	38 Baht
Phuket-Phang Nga	2 hr.	22 Baht
Phuket-Ranong	6 hr.	61 Baht (180 Baht air)

Local Transport

Buses

Buses leave daily for all the beaches from the market on Phang Nga Road in Phuket Town except those bound for Nai Han and Rawai Beach which leave from the traffic circle on Bangkok Road. Buses generally depart every 30 minutes between 8 am–5 pm. Fares are as follows from Phuket to:

Rawai	10 Baht	Kata, Karon	12 Baht
Patong	12 Baht	Koh Sire	8 Baht
Kamala	20 Baht	Surin	12 Baht
Sarasin	20 Baht	Nai Yang	20 Baht

Song Taew

Song Taews are the Phuket version of tuk-tuks. They carry up to five passengers. For destinations within Phuket Town they charge 5 Baht per person. From Phuket town to other destinations the one-way fares are as follows:

Rang Hill	30 Baht
Sire Island	40 Baht
Wat Chalong	50 Baht
Makham Bay	50 Baht
Chalong Bay	50 Baht
Laem Phrom Thep	120 Baht
Rawai Beach	80 Baht
Nai Han Beach	120 Baht
Kata Beach	100 Baht
Kata Noi Beach	120 Baht
Karon Beach	120 Baht
Patong Beach	100 Baht
Surin Beach	120 Baht
Tonsai Waterfall	120 Baht
Airport	150 Baht
Nai Yang Beach	160 Baht
Phang Nga	500 Baht

Boats

The only regularly scheduled boat service is from Ao Makham and Chalong Bay to Koh Phi Phi and Krabi. An express boat service, the Sea King, leaves from Makham Bay on Phuket for Krabi and Koh Phi Phi daily at 8:30 am. The 80 minute journey to Koh Phi Phi costs 250 Baht per person one-way.

Rentals

Auto Rentals

Automobiles, either jeeps or Toyota sedans, are available from several agencies on the island. Rates for sedans run around 1,200 Baht per day without petrol, and for jeeps 700 Baht per day without petrol. An international driver's licence and a deposit of around 1,000–2,000 Baht are required. Below is a list of some reliable agencies:

Hertz (6 locations)	tel. 311463
Avis (7 locations)	tel. 311358
Pure Car Rent	tel. 211002

Boat Rentals
Boats may be rented at Ao Chalong or Rawai beach. Generally a large boat seating 25 to 40 persons costs 1,000–5,000 Baht per day depending on the distances to be covered. Smaller boats of the 'long-tail' single screw variety (which carry up to 10 persons) cost 500–1,000 Baht a day. It should be stressed, however, that these smaller boats are not particularly seaworthy and should be avoided during the monsoon season when sudden storms are frequent. Be sure to bring hats, sunglasses and sun lotion as these boats usually are not covered. A luxury Chinese junk (as photographed on page 22) is available for rent through the Meridien Hotel, Phuket Yacht Club or Companies Generale du Siam in Bangkok, tel. 251-0225. The ship has four cabins which can sleep up to ten persons and costs US$1,000 per day. Below is a list of a few reputable charter services:

Phuket Yacht Charter	tel. 216556
South Asia Yacht Charter	tel. 321292
Thai Int'l Tour Co./Asia Voyage	tel. 216137, fax. 214668
Cruise Center	tel. 381793

Motorcycle Rentals

Motorcycles may be rented in Phuket Town along Rasada Rd. and are also available at Patong, Karon, Kata, Nai Han and Rawai Beaches. Rental rates vary according to the bike's horsepower, the range being generally 150–250 Baht per day without petrol. **Warning:** Motorcycles probably kill and injure more foreigners than any other hazard on Phuket. Drive defensively!

Useful Addresses and Phone Numbers

Emergency	
Tourist Police	199
Fire Brigade	212468
Ambulance	211111
Phuket Airport	212297
	311237 (Arivals)
Phuket Bus Terminal	311175 (Departures)
Local Telephone Information	211480
International Directory Assistance	13
Phuket's long distance area code	100
T.A.T (Tourist Authority of Thailand) 75–77 Phuket Rd.	(076)
Thai Airways Office Ranong Rd. near Fountain Circle	212213
Thai International Airways Office Montri Rd., near Clock Tower Circle	211195
Post Office	212880, 212855
Immigration	211020
	212108

Banks

Bangkok Bank	Phang Nga Rd.	211292
Bangkok Bank of Commerce	Phang Nga Rd.	212073
Krung Thai Bank	Yaowarat Rd.	211351
Ayudhaya Bank	Ratsada Rd.	212862
Thai Farmer's Bank	Phang Nga Rd.	212061
Thai Military Bank	Ranong Rd.	212123
Siam Commercial Bank	Ratsada Rd.	242638
Bangkok Metropolitan Bank	Montri Rd.	212993
Union Bank of Bangkok	Phuket Rd.	211501
Government Savings Bank	Phang Nga Rd.	211118
Bank of Asia	Phuket Rd.	211566

An unspoilt beach on Koh Phi Phi Island

Hospitals and Clinics

Mission Hospital	Thepkrasattri Rd.	211173
Siriroj Hospital	Krabi Road	215666
Phuket Ruamphaet	Phuket Rd.	216179
Wachira Hospital	Yaowaraj Rd.	211114
Andaman Hospital	Patong Beach	01 7230108
AR Clinic	Kata Beach	381590
OOS Dental Clinic	109/2 Phuket Rd. Phuket	212766

Restaurants (Cost per person exclusive of drinks: * less than 100 Baht
** 100–200 Baht
*** 200–400 Baht
**** over 400 Baht)

Phuket Town
  Tien Kung (Chinese)***
    Phuket Merlin Hotel   212866–70
  Erawan (Chinese seafood)**
    41/34 Montri Rd.   215299
  Jack and Joy (Thai)**
    118–120 Phang Nga Rd.   211838
  Kaw Yam (Thai, Bakery)*
    11/1 Thung Kaa Rd.   214201
  Khao Rung (Thai seafood)**
    Khao Rung Hill   —
  Krua-Thai (Thai)*
    62/7 Rasada Center   213479
  Le Café (French)*
    Rasada Center   215563
  Lucky Seafood Garden (Seafood)**
    66/1 Phuket Rd.   212175
  Miano (International)**
    54/10–11 Montri Rd.   214605
  Montree (Suki Yaki, soups)*
    Montree Hotel   212936
  On On Café (Budget Thai)*
    On On Hotel   —
  Phuket Seafood (Seafood)**
    66/2 Phuket Rd.   212245
  Phuket View Restaurant (Thai, Japanese)**
    Khao Rang Hill   216865
  Siang Chian (Chinese)**
    263–5 Talang Rd.   215928
  Suthep Roast Chicken (Thai chicken)**
    480 Phuket Rd.   216792
  Tong An (Chinese)***
    45–49 Phuket Rd.   211145
  Tunka Café (Thai)**
    Khao Rang Hilltop   211500
  Yama Kasa (Japanese)**
    95/15 Phuket Rd.   —

Patong Beach
  Mook Thong (Thai)**
    Baan Sukhothai Hotel   321195
  Regal Rendezvous (Seafood)**
    Thara Patong Beach Resort   321135

Savory (Seafood)*
  Safari Beach Hotel   321230-1
Baan Rim Pa (Thai classical)***
  100/7 Kalim Beach Rd.   017230386
Babylon (Italian)**
  93/12 Bangla Rd.   321156
Buffalo Steak House (Steak)***
  94/25-26 Soi Patong Resort   —
Chao Koh (Thai)*
  Soi Post Office   —
Da Rico Pizzeria (Pizza)**
  Soi Post Office   —
Paciugo (Ice cream)*
  Soi Patong Resort   —
Papagayo (French)**
  94/8 Soi Patong
  No. 4 Seafood (Seafood)**
  Bangla Rd.   —
Fondue and Steak House (Fondues)***
  94/20 Soi Patong Resort   321033
Grillhütte (German)**
  61/13-15 Patong Beach Rd.   321128
Patong Bay Inn (Seafood)**
  Thaweewong Rd.   321092
Patong Seafood (Seafood)**
  Thaweewong Rd.   321092
Riviera (French, Italian)****
  Holiday Inn   321020
Sabai-Sabai (Thai)*
  89/7 Soi Post Office   —
Shalimar (Indian)**
  89/59 Soi Post Office   017230488
The Living Place (Seafood)**
  Opp. Sai Namyen School   321121
Vecchia Venezia (Pizza)**
  82/16 Rat-u-thit Rd.   —

Karon and Karon Noi Beaches
Le Phuket (French)****
  Le Meridien Hotel, (Karon Noi)   321481-5
Napalai (Continental)***
  Karon Royal Wing Hotel   381139-49
Parichart Seafood Inn (Seafood)***
  Karon Villa   381139
Sakura (Japanese)***
  Karon Royal Wing Hotel   381139-48

San Sai Seafood (Seafood)***
   Thavorn Palm Beach Hotel   381034-7
Tai Kong (Steak and seafood)****
   Phuket Arcadia Hotel   381038 ext. 3080
Terrace (Italian)***
   Karon Bay Inn, Patak Rd.   —
Hayashi (Japanese)***
   Top of hill on Karon-Phuket Town Rd.   381710-4
Maxim's (Seafood)**
   Karon Beach Rd.   381500-2
Pa Ka Rang (Grill and coffee-house)***
   Crystal Beach Hotel   381580
Ristorante Italiano Pizzeria (Italian)**
   Karon Beach Rd.   —
Swiss Restaurant and Bakery (European)**
   Patak Rd. near Bougainvilla Apts.   381463

Kata and Kata Noi Beaches
Boathouse Inn (Thai, Western)***
   Boathouse Inn, Kata Beach   381557
Le Beaulieu (French)***
   Katathani Hotel, Kata Noi Beach   381124
Jack and Joy (Thai)*
   Opp. Kata Plaza, Kata Beach   —
Lobster and Prawn (Seafood)**
   Kata Center, Kata Beach   381619

Rawai Beach
Light House (French)****
   Phuket Island Resort   381010-7

Nai Han Beach
Chart Room Grill (French)****
   Phuket Yacht Club   381156

Cape Panwa
Top of the Reef (French)***
   Cape Panwa Sheraton   391123

Kamala Beach
Fisherman's Tavern (French Provencale)****
   Kamala Beach   017230379

Chalong Bay
Kan Eang (Seafood)**
   9/3 Chaofa Rd., Chalong Bay   381323

Night Entertainment

Discos
Banana Disco	Patong Beach Hotel	212841
Diamond Club Disco	Thavorn Hotel, Phuket	211333–5
Marina Disco Lounge	Merlin Hotel, Phuket	212866–70
Crocodile Music Hall	Soi Bangla, Patong	—

Cocktail Lounges and Massage Parlors
Bar Kho Yoy	Bangla Rd., Phuket	321176
Captain Bar Cocktail Lounge	Phuket Merlin Hotel	211618
Hong Thong Club	Phuket Rd. near Paradise	211070
Maikler Bar	Patong Beach	321118
Night Life	Pearl Hotel	211901–3
V.I.P. Cocktail Lounge	Phuket Rd., Phuket	
Pearl Massage Parlor	Pearl Hotel, Phuket	211901–3
Daeng Plaza Massage Parlor	Daeng Plaza Hotel, Phuket	—

Cinemas
Paradise Theatre	Phuket Rd., Phuket	211410
Pearl Cinema	Montri Rd., Phuket	211583
Pitak Cinema	Montri Road, Phuket	212112
Rengjit Cinema	Phuket Rd., Phuket	211520

Places of Worship

Takreng Christian Assembly	Chao Fa Road	Phuket
Roman Catholic Church	Soi Taling Chan,. Phuket Rd.	Phuket
Seventh Day Adventist Church	Thepkrasattri Rd.	Phuket
Dylyamiah Mosque	Soi Taling Chan, Phuket Rd.	Phuket
Suthat Rd. Mosque	Suthat Rd.	Phuket
Bang Tao Mosque	Surin Beach Rd.	Chengtalay

Water Sport Equipment, Supplies and Tours

Andaman Divers	Patong Beach	321155
Andaman Sea Sports	Phuket Town	211752
Diving Tours	Patong Beach	321141
Fantasea Divers	Patong Beach	321309
Ocean Divers	Patong Beach	321166
Phuket Aquatic Safaris	Phuket Town	216662
PEC Diving Centre	Phuket Town	215827
Phuket Divers	Phuket Town	215738
Santana Int'l Diving	Patong Beach	321360

Shopping

Supermarket and Department Stores:

Phuket Supermarket	Bangkok Rd.	
Phuket Foodland	Thalang Rd.	212975
Ocean Shopping Mall	Clock Tower Circle	211117
Phuket Foodland	Bangkok Rd.	211742

Photo Labs and Processing:

Charoen Slip	58/2 Ratsada Rd.	211075
Phuket Color Lab	1/7 Montri Rd.	215782
Patong Color Lab	87/23 Thawiwong Rd.	321382
P. Color Lab	38 Montri Rd.	216019
Phuket Art Photo	29/1 Phang-Nga Road	216470
Thida Computer Lab	46 Ratsada Rd.	216313

Lapidary (Gems, Pearls and Gold):

Mook Benjaporn	34 Montri Rd.	215809
Noppakao	69/71 Ratsada Rd.	212033
Phuket Pearl Gold Shop	159 Phang Nga Rd.	212419
Phuket Pearl Lapidary	51–53 Ratsada Rd.	211317
Yong Yoo Chang's Gold	Thalang Rd.	212051

Souvenir Shops

Coconut	87 Ratsada Rd.	212813
Nightingale Gift Shop	11/1 Phang Nga Rd.	212837
Nieces Souvenir	86/4 Thawiwong Rd.	321141
Ruk's Antique	7–9 Phang Nga Rd.	211434
Phuket Shell Shop	Road to Rawai Beach	216713
Phuket Souvenir Center	83-83/1 Ratsada Rd.	215381

Phuket Pewtercenter	52 Phuket Rd.	212639
Patong Goods Supplies	94/1 Thawiwong Rd.	321153
Pat Trades & Travels	86/4 Thawiwong Rd.	321258
Rawai Shell Product	91–93 Ratsada Rd.	211103
Sea World	77–79 Ratsada Rd.	211981
Sunshine Thai Products	89/1 Phuket Rd.	212889
Sea Pearl	89 Ratsada Rd.	215840
Thai Silk	48 Ratsada Rd.	215647

Bowling and Gold

Pearl Bowling	Phuket Rd., Phuket
Phuket Golf and Country Club	Kl. 6 Phuket-Patong Rd. tel. 213388

General books on Thailand

In this guide series is also published *A Guide to Thailand: Kingdom of Siam* by John Hoskin with photography by Michael Freeman. A very handy and useful illustrated guide which is distributed by the Asia Books company of Bangkok. It is also available in French, Italian and Dutch through Editions Olizane.

John Hoskin also authored *The Guide to Bangkok: City of Angels* and *A Buyer's Guide to Thai Gems and Jewellery* as well as *A Guide to Chiang-Mai and Northern Thailand* all of which are in the Asia Books Guide Series and available at all leading English language bookstores and hotels.

One of the best general guide books to the country is *Guide to Thailand* by Achille Clarac, published by the Duang Kamol Book House in Bangkok and Oxford University Press. Available in both French and English, this is particularly useful for anyone exploring Thailand by car as it contains precise information about distances as well as historical data.

For anyone interested in Thai arts and religious architecture, *The Arts of Thailand*, with a text by Steve Van Beek and photographs by Luca Invernizzi Tettoni (Travel Publishing Asia Ltd, Hong Kong) offers a comprehensive survey starting with the earliest period. The same publisher also issued a companion volume entitled *Legendary Thailand*, with a text by William Warren, dealing with cultural aspects of the country.

Thailand: a View From Above, published by Times Editions of Singapore, has spectacular aerial photographs by Luca Invernizzi Tettoni, some of them taken over Phuket and neighboring provinces, and a text by William Warren.

Thai Style, another production by Times Editions and distributed in

(Following page) *The dawn breaks gently over Krabi Island*

Thailand by Asia Books, deals with Thai homes, both traditional and modern; the text was written by William Warren and the photographs are by Luca Invernizzi Tettoni. One of the most striking contemporary homes featured in this book is located on Phuket.
Thailand's leading bookstores are those operated by the ASIA BOOKS Comp. (see credit page for office address). Their flagship store is located on Sukhumvit Rd. in Bangkok between Soi 15 and 17. Also in Bangkok they have two stores in the Landmark Hotel shopping plaza, one of which specializes in art and architecture books. The Landmark is also on Sukhumvit Rd. between Soi 4 and 6. Finally, there is another fine bookstore in the Peninsula Plaza next door to the Regent Hotel on Rajadamri Rd.

Other publications about Phuket

There have to date been only a handful of English language books devoted exclusively to Phuket. The finest volume on the market at this time (excluding our own publication of course!) is simply titled *Phuket* by Singapore-based travel writer, Fiona Nichols. This handsome, hard-backed 'mini-coffee table book' is published by Times Editions of Singapore and distributed by Asia Books in Thailand. Published in 1985, the book provides a pleasant general description of the island and its inhabitants.

Gerard Andre, former French ambassador to Thailand and currently a Phuket resident, wrote the forward to a 1987 publication by the Siam Society titled *Old Phuket*. The book reproduces an historical account of the island written by a Colonel Gerini and published originally in 1905. This book is an interesting and authoritative account of the island's history as perceived by an early foreign resident.

Another publication titled *Phuket* and published in both French and English (in the same volume) was written by a Monsieur Jean Boulbet some years ago and published by The Assumption Printing Press of Bangkok. Mr. Boulbet is a long term resident of Phuket. The slim (47 pages) softback volume is difficult to find but still one of the best general information sources on the island.

A peculiar little volume titled Phuket: *The Tropical Island as it Really Is* is published by Chalermnit Publications of Bangkok. The authors, Supatra Keawcum and Gottfried Richter, originally wrote the text in German which has been translated into English by the doyen of Thailand's publishing industry, Khun Manich Jumsai.

Another small handbook titled *A Guide to Phuket Island: Serendipity* seemingly anonymously published but written by Morag Mckerron consists largely of colorful advertisements with a brief text providing general information.

In a similar vein is the monthly *Guide to South Thailand* pubished by Shilpa Co. which is mostly an advertising medium for which you are expected to pay 60 Baht. These types of publication are usually free. The best map of Phuket is published by Panavongs Realty Co. and is now generally available in most of Phuket's bookstores. It features an interesting satellite image of Phuket Island as well as a detailed topographic outline of the island. It costs 150 Baht.

Basic Thai Vocabulary

Thai, like Chinese and various other more or less related languages and dialects in East and Southeast Asia, is a tonal, mostly monosyllabic language: that is, each spoken syllable can function on its own as a word, and has a certain pitch or intonation assigned to it which is as important in identifying it and distinguishing it from other words as the consonant and vowel sounds it is otherwise composed of. This aspect of the language makes it particularly difficult for speakers of non-tonal languages (including speakers of European languages) to learn. Complicating the picture even further is the Thai alphabet, based on (but yet different from) an ancient south Indian script. And there is no standard romanization system, resulting in a variety of spellings for even common place names: Ayutthaya/Ayudhaya, Chiang Mai/Chieng-mai, Chao Phraya/Chao Phya, etc.

Below is a short list of the words and phrases most easily and usefully learned by the short-term visitor. Even the most mangled attempt to speak Thai is welcomed with friendly laughter and encouragement, and is a good way to break the ice (and often bring down prices in shops and markets). For those who envision a more serious committment to learning Thai, dictionaries and phrase books are widely available; the truly devoted should contact the American University Alumni Association (A.U.A.), which runs a number of Thai and English language programs throughout the country. (A.U.A., 179 Rajdamri Road. Bangkok; tel. 252-7069.)

Numbers

one	neung
two	sorng
three	sam
four	see
five	haa
six	hok
seven	jet
eight	paet

nine	kao
ten	sip
eleven	sip-et
twelve	sip sorng
fifteen	sip haa
twenty	yee sip
twenty-one	yee sip-et
twenty-two	yee sip sorng
thirty	sam sip
fifty	haa sip
one hundred	neung roi
one thousand	neung paen
ten thousand	neung meun
one hundred thousand	neung saen
one million	neung laan

Basic Phrases

thank you	khawp khun khrap (male) khawp khun khaa (female)
hello, goodbye	sawat dee (khrap or khaa)
excuse me	khor thot
never mind	mai pen rai
no	mai
yes	chai (it is) or simply "khrap" or "kha"
how are you?	sabai dee reu?
I'm fine	sabai dee (khrap . . .)
I don't feel well	mai sabai (khrap . . .)

Questions and directions

what is your name?	khun cheu arai khrap?
my name is . . .	phom (male) chun (female) cheu . . .
where is . . .	you nai?
I want to go to . . .	yaak ja pai . . .
turn left	leou sai
turn right	leou khwa
straight ahead	trong pai
stop here	yoot tee nee
how much does this cost?	nee baht taw rai?

Places

hotel	rawng ram
street	tanon
side street	soi
bus station	sat-hani rot meh
railway station	sat-hani rot fai
airport	sanam bin (in Bangkok 'Don Muang')
city	nakhon
town	muang
village	ban
beach	haat
island	koh
mountain, hill	doi, khao
restaurant	raan ahaan
hospital	rong phaya-bahn
post office	prai-sannee
police station	sat-hani tamruat
embassy	sat-han toot
bathroom	hawng nam
room	hawng
market	talatt
river	menam
nation	prahtett

Useful words

today	wan nee
yesterday	meua wan nee
tomorrow	proong nee
day	wan
week	ahtit
month	deun
year	pee
hungry	hew kao
thirsty	hew nam
food	ahahn
water	nam
train	rot fai
auto	rot yon
boat	reua
airplane	kreung bin
taxi	taksee

Food

water	nam
salt	kreua
sugar, sweet	wan
chilli pepper	plik
beef	neua
pork	moo
chicken	gai
eggs	kai
fish	plaa
vegetables	pahk
fruit	pohlamai
rice	khao
to eat	khao
to drink	deum
soup	tom
coffee	cafe
tea	cha

Index

Adang, 92
Amanpuri Resort, 32
Ao Luk, 77
Ao Luk Bay, 63, 77
Ao Phra Nang, 91
Aquarium, 53
Asalha Bucha, 109

Baan Niew, 113
Ban Kosol Bungalow, 34
Bang Neow Temple, 113
Bang Tao Beach, 30
Bang Tao Mosque, 58
Beaches, 29–46
Bird's Nest Caves, 26, 68, 73
Bird's Nest Soup, 26, 69–73
Boathouse Inn, 43
Boxing, 55
Boxing Stadium, 55
Buddhist Lent, 109

Cape Panwa Sheraton, 46
Capricorn Bungalow, 34
Chakri Day, 107
Chalong Bay, 53
Chinese New Year, 107
Chinese Temples, 55
Chulalongkron Day, 109
Club Andaman, 34
Club Mediterranee, 43
Coconut Villa, 34
Constitution Day, 112
Coral Beach Hotel, 34
Coronation Day, 109

Diamond Cliff Resort, 34
District Office, 24
Dusit Laguna Hotel, 30

Festivals, 107–114
Fruits, 26, 93–100

Food, 102–103

Gang Mussaman, 102
Government House, 47

Hat Noppharat Thara, 91
Her Majesty Queen Sirikit's Birthday, 109
His Majesty King Bhumibol Adulyadej's Birthday, 112
Heroine's Monument, 22, 55
Ho Mok, 103
Holiday Inn, 34
Holiday Resort, 36
Holidays, 107–114
Hyashi Thai House, 43

Jui Tui Temple, 113

Kakata Inn '85', or Kata Inn, or Kata Inn '85', 40
Kamala Beach, 32
Kanom Chin, 102
Karon Beach, 40–41
Karon Noi, or Relax Bay, 40
Karon Villa/Karon Royal Wing, 40
Karon Yai, 40
Kata Beach, 43–44
Kata Noi, 43, 44
Kata Villa, 40
Kata Yai, 43
Katathani Hotel, 44
Kathu, 55
Khanab Num Mount, 91
Khao Chang, 63
Khao Khian, 77
Khao Phra Thaeo, 24
Khao Phra Thaeo National Park, 49–53
Khao Phingkan, or James Bond Island, 77

Khao Rang, 49
Khatu District, 112
Khatu Temple, 112, 113
Koh Kaeo, 53
Koh Chong Lat, 77
Koh Hi, or Coral Island 82
Koh Klui, 77
Koh Mai Thong, 82
Koh Mak, 77
Koh Nakha Noi, 82, 86
Koh Nakha Yai, 82
Koh Pannyi, 77, 80
Koh Phi Phi Don, 64
Koh Phi Phi Le, 64–68, 73
Koh Sire, 55, 106
Koh Yai Noi, 77
Koh Yai Yai, 77
Krabi, 63, 88–90
Krabi Resort, 88

Laem Ka Beach Inn, 44
Laem Phrom Thep, 53
Lak Muang, 22, 53–55
Lawa Yai Island, 82
Le Meridien Hotel, or 'Relax Bay Resort', 40
Lone Island Resort, 46
Loy Krathong, 109
Loy Rua Festival, 55

Mai Khao Beach, 30
Makha Bucha, 107
Marina Cottage, 40
Marine Biological Researc Centre, 58, 114
Mee Hokkian, 103
Miang Island, 88
Mission Hospital, 15
Muslim Villages, 55–58

Nai Han Beach, 44
Nai Thon Beach, 30
Nai Yang Beach, 30

Nam Pia, 102
Namphrik Kung Siap, 103
Naowarat Hotel, 88
New Year's Eve, 107

Og Phansa, 109
On On Hotel, 49

Panorama Beach Club, 36
Pansea Beach, 32
Pansea Hotel, 32
Paradise Bungalow, 36
Patong Bay Garden Resort, or Patong Bay Hotel, 36
Patong Bay Inn, 36
Patong Bayshore Hotel, 36
Patong Beach, 34–37
Patong Beach Hotel, 36
Patong Lodge Hotel, 36
Patong Merlin Hotel, 36
Patong Resort, 36
Patong Villa, 37
Pearl farming, 82, 85–86
Pearl Hotel, 49
Pearl Village Beach Hotel, 30
Phang Nga, 63
Phang Nga Bay, 63, 75–77
Phang Nga Bay National Park, 75
Phang Nga Bay Resort, 63, 75
Phi Phi Islands, 64–68
Phi Phi Island Cabana, 90
Phi Phi Island Hotels, 90
Phi Phi Village, 90
Phuket Arcadia Hotel, 41
Phuket Cabana, 37
Phuket Golden Sand Inn, 41
Phuket Golf and Country Club, 55
Phuket Island Resort, 46
Phuket Kamala Resort, 32
Phuket Merlin Hotel, 49
Phuket Museum, 53
Phuket Ocean Resort, 41
Phuket Ruamphaet Hospital, 15

Phuket Sea Shell, 15
Phuket Town, 47–49
Phuket Yacht Club, 44
Plants, 26, 93–100
Port of Phuket, 49
PP International Resort, 90
Provincial Court, 47
Put Jaw Temple, 55

Rasada Street Market, 49
Rawai Beach, 44–46, 106
Rawai Plaza and Bungalow, 44
Rawai Resort Hotel, 46

Safari Beach Hotel, 37
Sapan Hin, or Stone Bridge, 55, 113
Sea Gypsy Village, 55, 104-106
Seagull Cottage, 37
Seaview Hotel, 37
Sepum, 106
Similan Islands, 88
Siriroj Hotel, 15
Skandia Bungalows, 37
Songkran, or Thai New Year, 107
Su San Hoi, or Shell Cemetery Beach, 90
Sua Cave, 91
Surin Beach, 32
Suwannakuha, 63

Tarutao National Park, 92
Tha Rua, 55
Tham Khao, 77
Tham Lot, 77
Tham Phi Hua To, 91
Tham Russi, 63
Tham Sadet, 91
Than Bok Khoran, 91
Than Bok Koroni National Park, 63
Thara Patong, 37
Thavorn Palm Beach Hotel, 41
Tone Sai Waterfall, 53
Tropica Bungalows Hotel, 37

Turtle Release Festival, 114

Vegetarian Festival, 109, 112–114
Visaka Bucha, 108

Wat Chalong, 53
Wat Phra Thong, 53
Wat Tham Sua, or Tiger Cave Monastery, 91
Wiang Thong, 90

Yupadeewan Nursery, 55, 90
Yupadeewan Nursery, 55

APGB/15-03